Studies in Outdoor Recreation

Search and Research for Satisfaction

Studies in Outdoor Recreation
Search and Research for Satisfaction

Robert E. Manning

Oregon State University Press
Corvallis, Oregon

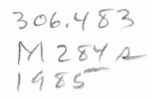

The paper in this book meets the guidelines for permanence and durability of the Committee on Production Guidelines for Book Longevity of the Council on Library Resources.

Library of Congress Cataloging in Publication Data

Manning, Robert E., 1946-
  Studies in outdoor recreation.

  Bibliography: p.
  Includes index.
  1. Outdoor recreation—Research—Evaluation.
I. Title.
GV191.6.M314   1985   306'.483   85-15447
ISBN 0-87071-344-2
ISBN 0-87071-345-0 (pbk.)

Preface

In the early 1970s a haunting paper was published in the outdoor recreation literature pointedly titled "Recreation Research—So What?" The authors of that paper questioned the significance of outdoor recreation research. This book attempts to answer their question.

This study is primarily a review and synthesis of social science literature in outdoor recreation. A large number of conceptual and empirically-based studies in outdoor recreation have been conducted over the past two decades. However, these studies have been highly diverse in disciplinary approach and methods, and widely dispersed over space and time. Little systematic effort has been devoted to integrating these studies into a body of knowledge. This study attempts to develop and present a state-of-the-art body of knowledge on major outdoor recreation management and research issues.

I am grateful to many people and organizations for helping make this study possible. Such a study requires an extended period of time to read and write, and this was made possible in large part through the generous sabbatical program of the University of Vermont. I am particularly grateful to Dr. Hugo John, past Dean, and Dr. Lawrence Forcier, current Dean of the School of Natural Resources, for their encouragement and support.

My feeling was that a national park would be a suitable setting in which to conduct this study. Fortunately, the National Park Service agreed, and arrangements were made for me to spend the sabbatical year at Grand Canyon National Park. Special thanks are expressed to Richard Marks, Superintendent, and Steve Hodapp, Chief of Resources Management, for their professional and personal hospitality. Deep appreciation is also expressed to the Grand Canyon Natural History Association for partial funding of this study.

The study required gathering many publications not in my possession. This was greatly facilitated by the kindness of Northern Arizona University which granted me a Visiting Professorship, providing me access to their fine library. In particular, I thank Dr. Richard Behan, Dean of the School of Forestry, for this professional courtesy. The staff of Bailey/Howe Library at the University of Vermont was also very helpful in processing interlibrary loan requests.

Two people were particularly helpful with the technical aspects of preparing the book. Sherry Churchill patiently typed and retyped the manuscript. Jo Alexander, Managing Editor of the Oregon State University Press, skillfully edited the manuscript and provided many helpful suggestions.

Contents

Chapter Eight
Managing Outdoor Recreation:

Chapter Nine
Managing Outdoor Recreation:

List of Tables

List of Figures

Chapter One
Search for Satisfaction: An Introduction to Outdoor Recreation Research

Objectives of the Book

The purpose of this book is to review and synthesize the research-based literature on social science aspects of outdoor recreation. While social science research in outdoor recreation has a limited history, the number of studies has grown dramatically in recent years. However, with the exception of normally cursory literature review sections at the beginning of most published papers, little formal effort has been aimed at integrating this emerging body of knowledge.

The need for this study is apparent for several reasons, all stemming from the inherent diversity of the field of outdoor recreation. First and foremost is the multidisciplinary nature of the subject itself. Issues in outdoor recreation are conventionally dichotomized into ecological concerns (e.g. environmental impacts) and social science concerns (e.g. crowding and conflicting uses). But even within the social science domain, issues may be approached from a variety of disciplinary perspectives including sociology, psychology, geography, political science, and economics. Integration of these discipline-based studies can be complex. Indeed, simply locating the research in the variety of journals and other publication sources in which it is reported can be difficult. Outdoor recreation research also tends to be isolated in space and time—studies are widely scattered geographically and are conducted over varying time periods. At least on the surface, an early study of developed campgrounds in an eastern park can be difficult to integrate with a more recent study of wilderness use in the west. Yet they are both studies in outdoor recreation and will doubtless contribute more to the body of knowledge when synthesized than in isolation. Finally, outdoor recreation has been subject to wide methodological diversity. Even though the dominant research approach has been to survey on-site visitors, there has been wide variation in sampling techniques, the scope of such studies, and the way in which important variables have been operationalized. Attempts to integrate studies are often frustrated by these inconsistencies. Still, the basic thrust of such studies can often be brought together to build evidence for or against a relationship, hypothesis, or theory. Moreover, a large-scale synthesis is likely to highlight methodological inconsistencies and hopefully enhance the direct comparability of future research.

One result of this book, it is hoped, is a response to the frequent criticism that outdoor recreation research has few practical implications (e.g. Brown et al. 1973). Applied to each study individually, this observation is largely true. But in a broad and interdisciplinary field such as outdoor recreation, this is probably how it should and must be. The essence of the scientific method is to divide issues into small and manageable components for study. Only after a critical mass of knowledge has been created in this manner can the synergistic effects of the research process begin to develop. The body of knowledge then becomes more than the sum of its parts. In this book, the findings from a large number of studies are synthesized into knowledge and understanding. In this manner, the management implications begin to become apparent.

The book is organized in nine chapters, most of which focus on a major theme in the literature. Though the book is divided primarily by subject matter, it also has an historical bent. Emphasis on one theme often evolves from development of another. The research on crowding of the late 1970s, for example, has its roots in the concept of carrying capacity explored in the previous decade. In addition, the development of most new fields of study follows a similar pattern as they evolve from basic descriptive approaches to more explanatory and analytical efforts. This pattern is reflected throughout the course of the book.

The first chapter briefly reviews the history of social science research in outdoor recreation and notes the emphasis on establishing and maintaining satisfaction among visitors, though definitions of satisfaction have changed over time. Chapters Two and Three focus on the early social and descriptive studies. Topics included are some of the most basic issues in outdoor recreation: recreation activity patterns, social and cultural influences on recreation participation, and the attitudes, preferences, and perceptions of visitors to outdoor recreation areas. Chapter Four examines the adoption of carrying capacity as an organizing framework in outdoor recreation. Borrowed from the biological sciences of wildlife and range management, the concept of carrying capacity has been found useful in the field of outdoor recreation, but only after extensive modification. A central tenet of recreation carrying capacity suggests that satisfaction of visitors will decline with increasing use density. The large group of studies exploring the relationship between density and satisfaction is the focus of Chapter Five. The sixth chapter examines motivations for outdoor recreation. The evolution of outdoor recreation research from a descriptive to an explanatory phase is perhaps seen most clearly in the studies reviewed in Chapters Five and Six. The most recent theme to emerge in the outdoor recreation literature is the notion of diversity. If there has been one clearly recurring conclusion in the literature, it is that public tastes in outdoor recreation are diverse. Chapter Seven reviews several conceptual systems designed to ensure diversity in outdoor recreation, including the recently developed Recreation Opportunity Spectrum. Chapter Eight examines strategies and tactics for managing outdoor recreation. A variety of management alternatives are presented and evaluated. The final chapter focuses directly on management implications of the body of knowledge developed in outdoor recreation research. Whereas Chapters Two through Eight outline what is currently known about basic outdoor recreation concepts, Chapter Nine applies this body of knowledge in developing a series of principles of outdoor recreation and a process for planning and managing outdoor recreation areas. It should be emphasized that what is developed is a process rather than a prescription.

Like all studies, the review and synthesis reported in this book have limits. Though the study is multidisciplinary within the social sciences, the theoretical perspectives are drawn primarily from sociology, psychology, geography and, to a limited extent, economics. This is more a reflection of the literature itself than conscious selection. Similarly, the study covers the time period from the early 1960s through the present; this is primarily a function of when outdoor recreation research activity has occurred. The emphasis of the study is on published research. Confidence in research findings is enhanced when they have seen the light of critical review, and these materials are more generally available. Finally, the study is oriented to the public sector of outdoor recreation.

Research in Outdoor Recreation

Outdoor recreation is not a discipline in the conventional academic sense; that is, it is not a basic branch of knowledge like biology, mathematics, or sociology. It is an applied field of study focused on an issue or problem which has attracted the attention of a broad segment of society. Though research in outdoor recreation can be traced back fifty years or more (e.g. Meinecke 1928; Bates 1935), sufficient attention was not focused on outdoor recreation for it to emerge as a field of study until after World War II. During the 1950s rapid gains in economic prosperity, ease of transportation, leisure time, and other social forces conspired to produce dramatic and sustained increases in the use of outdoor recreation areas. Problems in the form of environmental impacts and crowding began to attract the attention of both professionals and the public as manifested in articles such as Bernard Devoto's *Let's Close the National Parks* (1953) and Marion Clawson's *The Crisis in Outdoor Recreation* (1959). Outdoor recreation as a field of study was born in this period.

Most observers date the beginning of serious social scientific study of this field to the publication of the Outdoor Recreation Resources Review Commission (ORRRC) reports. The ORRRC was a presidential commission established in 1958 to assess the status of outdoor recreation in America. It published its widely read summary report, *Outdoor Recreation for America*, in 1962 along with 29 special studies. The paucity of outdoor recreation research prior to that time is evident in one of the special studies which surveyed the outdoor recreation literature. The introduction to the report stated:

> The outline prepared as a guide for the bibliographic search assumed the existence of a substantial body of material relating rather directly to

outdoor recreation. As the actual hunt progressed, the true situation—that the field (if it is yet that) of outdoor recreation has been but sketchily treated—became more and more evident (Librarian of Congress 1962, p. 2).

The card catalog of the Library of Congress, the central source for any bibliographer, had no subject heading, "outdoor recreation." Fewer than ten entries were found which referred definitely to outdoor recreation in their titles.

Most of the early research in outdoor recreation was biological or ecological. This was due, at least in part, to the fact that most outdoor recreation managers were professionally trained in the traditional biological disciplines (Lime 1972a; Hendee and Stankey 1973). As early as 1934 Lundberg et al. observed that social scientists had paid little attention to the problem of leisure. The multidisciplinary nature of outdoor recreation, however, gained recognition in the post-World War II period. Social problems such as crowding began to supplement traditional concerns for environmental impacts, and participants in outdoor recreation activities were recognized as having socio-economic characteristics, attitudes, and preferences which might be of interest and use to resource managers. Emphasis on the social aspects of outdoor recreation was furthered in the 1960s and early 1970s by a series of calls for research on outdoor recreation in several major social science disciplines: sociology (Catton 1971; Hendee 1971), economics (Clawson and Knetsch 1963), psychology (Driver 1972), geography (Mitchell 1969), and a general multidisciplinary approach (Lucas 1966).

Early social science research in outdoor recreation and leisure in general was primarily descriptive, focusing on the activities and social characteristics of participants. Berger, for example, observed in this early period that:

> The sociology of leisure today is little else than a reporting of survey data on what selected samples of individuals do with the time in which they are not working and the correlation of these data with conventional demographic variables. There are several important exceptions to this general statement, but they do not alter the melancholy fact that empirical proof that rich people play polo more often than poor people gives us little reason to hope that an incipient sociology of leisure is taking shape (Berger 1962, p. 37).

Certainly, many of the ORRRC studies fall into this general pattern. A related criticism of this early period was that research efforts generally lacked a conceptual or theoretical foundation. Meyersohn (1969), for example, characterized most studies as "sheer empiricism."

But these criticisms could be made of any developing field of study. Initial research is inevitably descriptive and exploratory. Though some contemporary studies might still fall into these categories, the field of outdoor recreation research advanced relatively rapidly. In 1970 Moncrief noted that the field was beginning to move beyond the descriptive phase and into more sophisticated explanatory studies. Field and Cheek introduced their paper in 1974 by noting that "in the investigation of any problem area there must be a systematic and rigorous effort by many so that studies are progressive and research findings are accumulative, if a critical mass of theoretical and substantive knowledge is to emerge." They concluded that "In the study of leisure, we are coming of age" (Field and Cheek 1974). The same year, Burdge reached a similar conclusion: "The study of leisure is approaching the threshold of real accomplishment" (Burdge 1974).

These observations seem to be borne out by the literature reviewed in this book. While much of the early literature outlined in Chapters Two and Three is descriptive, more recent studies—the focus of later chapters—explore the theoretical constructs of carrying capacity, crowding, motivations for recreation, and diversity.

If the quality of outdoor recreation research is debatable, certainly the quantity is not. Just eleven years after the scant literature base of the ORRRC studies, Stankey and Lime (1973) developed a bibliography on outdoor recreation carrying capacity containing 208 citations. And a 1978 bibliography on the narrower subject of river recreation (Anderson et al.) contained 355 citations. A recent bibliography on recreation research publications through 1982 by U.S. Forest Service scientists and their cooperators contains 932 entries (Echelberger et al. 1983a).

Burdge (1983) has offered a recent analysis of outdoor recreation research based on study of the two leading research-based journals of the field, the *Journal of Leisure Research* and *Leisure Sciences*. Study of authors and editors of these journals reveals a trend away from a disciplinary approach to outdoor recreation to a more multidisciplinary treatment. Contributions from the traditional social science disciplines of sociology, psychology, and economics have declined in the recent period relative to contributions from researchers in the broader park, recreation, and related departments, whose studies are broader in nature and more appropriate to problem solving in an inherently multidisciplinary field.

Research in outdoor recreation has, then, evolved in the classic manner of most emerging fields of study. Most early studies were descriptive and exploratory, substituting data for theory. An expanding data base allowed more conceptual and analytical development, and then a multidisciplinary approach. These trends are evident in the scholarly journals in which studies are reported. The early studies of the 1950s and 1960s are found in the journals of sociology, psychology, economics, and forestry. As research activity expanded, the developing field of outdoor recreation created its own scholarly publication outlets, including the *Journal of Leisure Research* in 1969 and *Leisure Sciences* in 1977. Evolution of the field is continuing as more specialized interests splinter off and are served by their own journals; examples include the *Therapeutic Recreation Journal* and the *Journal of Park and Recreation Administration*.

Quality in Outdoor Recreation:
Search and Research for Satisfaction

As in most other areas of life, "quality" has been the underlying goal of those involved in outdoor recreation. Managers certainly want to provide high quality outdoor recreation environments, and visitors want to have high quality outdoor recreation experiences. As a consequence, the concept of quality is contained, explicitly or implicitly, in the goals and policies governing most outdoor recreation areas. But what is quality in outdoor recreation? One researcher has recently suggested that it is a less valid goal than generally supposed:

> As a useful goal, it is just clear enough to be professionally embraced and just fuzzy enough to go unchallenged as to its meaning (LaPage 1983, p. 279).

The principal measure of quality in outdoor recreation has long been defined by visitor satisfaction. Beginning with the ORRRC studies, quality in outdoor recreation was measured by user satisfaction (Department of Resource Development 1962). LaPage (1963) argued that satisfaction was the appropriate measure of the "recreational productivity" of outdoor sites. Satisfaction as a goal in outdoor recreation has been confirmed and reconfirmed throughout the literature:

> Providing recreation opportunities . . . for the constructive and satisfying use of leisure by all the nation's people is a primary public purpose (National Academy of Sciences 1969, p. 1).

> . . . human satisfaction stands as the ultimate goal of resource programs directed toward providing camping opportunities (Bultena and Klessig 1969, p. 348).

> . . . the principal goal of recreation management is to maximize user satisfaction consistent with certain administrative, budgetary, and resource constraints (Lime and Stankey 1971, p. 175).

> . . . we assume the goal of recreation management is to maximize user satisfaction (Lucas and Stankey 1974, p. 14).

> The objective of recreation management . . . is to maximize user satisfaction within specified constraints of budget or physical resource or agency policy (Bury 1976, p. 23).

> In recent years . . . perhaps the most widely used conception of recreation quality has been that of satisfaction (More and Buyhoff 1979, p. 1).

The focus on satisfaction arises out of the need for some evaluative communication between visitors and managers. Because outdoor recreation in the public sector is traditionally priced free or at a nominal level, managers generally lack the clear feedback mechanism available in the private sector in the form of "price signals." Most managers recognize the potential usefulness of visitor opinions, within the constraints of resource and management factors, in meeting the quality objectives of outdoor recreation areas.

Attempts at measuring satisfaction, however, have met with several complications. Overall measures of satisfaction may be too broad to be useful. Satisfaction is a multidimensional concept, affected by a number of parameters, some under the control of managers and many not. Measures of overall satisfaction may not be sensitive enough to detect changes in the few parameters of interest to managers. It has been suggested that satisfaction with an outdoor recreation opportunity may vary with any of the three basic factors which define such opportunities: 1) the physical and biological characteristics of the site; 2) the type and level of management action; and 3) the social and cultural characteristics of the visitor (Propst and Lime 1982).

This last factor has particularly important implications for using satisfaction as a measure of quality. Satisfaction may depend on visitors and their perceptions of an area as much as, or more than, on the characteristics of the area itself. While changes in visitor satisfaction may be found over time, it is suggested that these changes be interpreted:

> not as a *measure* of real change in services, but as an *indicator* of perceived change. The indicator may be a valid expression of physical change, changes in perception, changes in clientele and their expectations, or all three in combination. Therefore, changes in satisfaction scores can only be realistically used as clues that some element of . . . management may need more (or less) management attention (LaPage and Bevins 1981, p. 5).

The importance of individual perceptions in determining satisfaction has been documented not only in outdoor recreation, but in other facets of the quality of life as well: job satisfaction, satisfaction with one's community, and satisfaction in marriage (Shelby et al. 1980).

One of the most commonly recurring themes in outdoor recreation literature is that visitors to outdoor recreation areas often differ in ways that fundamentally affect satisfaction and perceptions of quality. Visitors have different socio-economic characteristics, are exposed to different cultural influences, and have widely varying attitudes, preferences, and motivations. Therefore, visitors' relatively high ratings of satisfaction with recreation sites may simply reflect a changing visitor population rather than high quality. High satisfaction may be as much a function of high demand for all types of outdoor recreation opportunities as it is of good management.

Recognition of varying tastes in outdoor recreation has led to a new thrust in defining and measuring quality, one equated with diversity itself. Outdoor recreation might best be viewed as a system of opportunities providing a wide variety of experiences. Each opportunity within the system should be planned and managed explicitly for the experiences most appropriate for that area. Goals and objectives governing the area would be changed only by conscious decision, not by a process of creeping incrementalism possible under general satisfaction monitoring. Under this interpretation, quality in outdoor recreation is defined as the degree to which each opportunity satisfies the experiences for which it is planned and managed. In this way, total satisfaction of all outdoor recreationists might truly be maximized.

The evolution of the concept of quality in outdoor recreation and the search and research for visitor satisfaction is traced in detail in the following chapters.

Summary and Conclusions

1. *The purpose of this book is to review and synthesize the research-based literature on social science aspects of outdoor recreation.*

2. *The need for this study stems from the multidisciplinary nature of outdoor recreation and the spatial, temporal, and methodological diversity of research.*

3. *Management implications of outdoor recreation become more evident when studies are integrated into a body of knowledge.*

4. *The first eight chapters of the book focus on major themes in the literature, and present a state-of-the-art knowledge of basic outdoor recreation concepts. The final chapter applies this body of knowledge in developing a process for planning and managing outdoor recreation areas.*

5. *Outdoor recreation is not an academic discipline but an interdisciplinary, applied field of study.*

6. *Research in outdoor recreation, particularly empirically-based social science study, began in earnest in the early 1960s when outdoor recreation was recognized as important and potentially problematic by a broad segment of society. Research has expanded greatly in recent years.*

7. *Outdoor recreation research has evolved in the classic pattern of developing fields of study. Early studies tended to be descriptive, exploratory, and disciplinary-based, while more recent studies have tended to be conceptually-based, explanatory, and multidisciplinary.*

8. *Quality is the underlying goal of outdoor recreation, but efforts to measure quality in terms of visitor satisfaction have met with several difficulties, including the multi-dimensional nature of satisfaction and diversity in tastes for outdoor recreation.*

9. *Quality in outdoor recreation has evolved from overall measures of satisfaction to the degree to which outdoor recreation opportunities satisfy the experiences for which they are planned and managed.*

Chapter Two
Social Aspects of Outdoor Recreation: Use and Users

Recreation Use and Users

Information on recreation use and users was recognized early as potentially important for a number of reasons. Bury, for example, suggested in 1964 several ways relatively simple data from campground registration forms might be useful in the planning and design of recreation facilities. Information on size of camping groups, for instance, can be important to campground designers.

As this base of information has grown, so has its application. Several more recent writers (Lime and Buchman 1974; Plumley et al. 1978; Knopf and Lime 1984) have developed extended guides illustrating the ways in which information on recreation use and the characteristics of users can and should be integrated into recreation management. Applications range from monitoring the popularity of recreation activities so as to more efficiently plan budgetary, personnel and other resource needs to determining the residence and education level of users in order to more effectively conduct public information and education programs.

A related issue concerns the desirability of collecting this type of information on a regular basis. As societal conditions change, so do recreation patterns. Graphic illustration of these changes is highlighted in a comparison of five recreation use studies conducted over a 25-year period at Yosemite National Park (Van Wagtendonk 1980). Average length of stay, for example, declined from 2.34 days to 1.32 days reflecting a substantial increase in day use. Day users and other short-term visitors have different facility and service needs, and these should be reflected in management programs. A series of research and management conferences has developed to focus on this type of trend information (LaPage 1980).

This and the following chapter examine social and descriptive aspects of outdoor recreation. This chapter focuses on measures of recreation activity and characteristics of recreationists. Chapter Three considers attitudes, preferences, and perceptions of visitors to outdoor recreation areas.

Outdoor Recreation Activity

The first and simplest form of research into social aspects of outdoor recreation was use measurement. Initial efforts, going back for some areas and agencies well before World War II, were primarily simple headcounts of visitors to recreation areas. Later efforts became more sophisticated, including length-of-stay measures and categorization of visits by specific activities such as camping and hiking.

Use measurement is often difficult due to the dispersed nature of outdoor recreation activity. A number of studies beginning in the 1960s developed and evaluated various use sampling procedures.[1] A variety of relatively sophisticated use sampling and measurement techniques have been developed, including mechanical and electronic counting devices, optical scanners and cameras, direct and indirect observation, and self-administered, personal interview, telephone and mail surveys.

Many recreation agencies have developed relatively standard use measurement procedures based on these techniques. But there are often substantive differences between agencies. Figure 2-1, for example, shows annual use of areas administered by the five major federal outdoor recreation agencies. But these data include at least three measurement units—recreation days, recreation visits, and recreation visitor-days. A recreation day is the presence of a visitor in a recreation area for any part of a calendar day. A recreation visit is the entry of a visitor into a recreation area and has no relation to length of stay. A recreation visitor-day is the presence of a visitor in a recreation area for 12 hours or any combination of visitors and hours that equals 12. These differences in use measurement confound efforts to compare use between areas and sometimes even over time as agencies change use measurement procedures.

Household surveys are a potentially more useful approach to measuring outdoor recreation because they are more likely to be representative of recreation participation patterns of the general population than are on-site studies. The first large scale household survey in the field was conducted in 1960 as part of the ORRRC studies, and was a nationwide survey among persons 18 years and older (Ferriss 1962). The purpose of this survey was to determine the relative popularity of outdoor recreation activities as a guide to establishing priorities for further development. The federal government has conducted periodic similar nationwide surveys as part of its outdoor recreation planning process. Summary results for each of the four major nationwide surveys are shown in Table 2-1. In addition, the Land and Water Conservation Fund Act of 1964 required states to conduct comprehensive recreation planning to qualify for matching federal grants. Many states conducted household surveys patterned after the federal studies as a part of their planning process.

---

[1] Some of these studies are Bury and Hall 1963; James and Ripley 1963; Wenger 1964; Bury and Margolis 1964; Wenger and Gregersen 1964; James and Rich 1966; James and Tyre 1967; James 1968; James and Henley 1968; Wagar 1969; Wagar and Thalheimer 1969; Elsner 1970; Cordell and James 1970; James 1971; James and Schreuder 1971; Lucas et al. 1971; James et al. 1971a; James et al. 1971b; James and Schreuder 1972; James and Quinkert 1972; Marnell 1977; Hogans 1978; More 1980; Leonard et al. 1980.

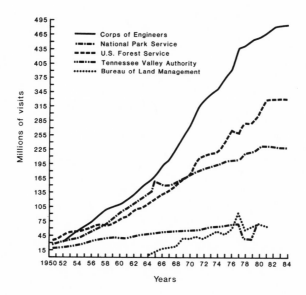

Corps of Engineers. Data, which are not available prior to 1952, are recreation days. A recreation day represents one person entering an area to pursue one or more recreation activities during a 24-hour period.

National Park Service. From 1950 to 1959, recreation visits are graphed. A recreation visit refers to entry by a person into a recreation area or site to carry on one or more recreation activities. From 1960 to 1984, visits are graphed. A visit refers to entry of any person into an area administered by the National Park Service such that he or she makes some use of the services or facilities provided therein.

U.S. Forest Service. From 1950 to 1964, recreation visits (same definition as National Park Service) are graphed. From 1965 to 1984, recreation visitor days are graphed. A recreation visitor day is defined as recreational use of an area which aggregates 12 person-hours. Any combination of people and time, either continuous or intermittent, which aggregates as 12 person-hours is considered a recreation visitor day.

Tennessee Valley Authority. Recreation visits (same definition as National Park Service) are graphed. Data are not available after 1980.

Bureau of Land Management. Data, which are not available prior to 1964, are graphed in terms of recreation visitor days (same definition as U.S. Forest Service). Recreation visitor hours were measured after 1981. A recreation visitor hour is defined as the presence of a person in a recreation area or site for the purpose of engaging in recreation activities during continuous, intermittent, or simultaneous periods of time aggregating 60 minutes. Due to their lack of comparability with recreation visitor days, these data are not graphed.

Figure 2-1.   Recreation use at areas administered by five major federal outdoor recreation agencies, 1950-1984. (Adapted from Driver and Rosenthal 1982)

Table 2-1. Nationwide participation rates in selected outdoor recreation activities, 1960-1977.

	1960[a]	1965[b]	1972[c]	1977[d]
	Percent participating			
Picnicking	53	57	47	72
Driving for pleasure	52	55	34	69
Sightseeing	42	49	37	62
Swimming	45	48		
Pool	--	--	18	63
Other	--	--	34	46
Walking and jogging	33	48	34	68
Playing outdoor games	30	38	22	56
Golf	--	9	5	16
Tennis	--	16	5	33
Fishing	29	30	24	53
Attending outdoor sports events	24	30	12	61
Other boating	22	24	15	34
Bicycling	9	16	10	47
Nature walks	14	14	17	50
Bird watching	--	5	4	--
Wildlife photography	--	2	2	--
Attending outdoor concerts, plays	9	11	7	41
Camping	8	10	--	--
Developed	--	--	11	30
Backcountry	--	--	5	21
Horseback riding	6	8	5	15
Hiking or backpacking	6	7	5	28
Waterskiing	6	6	5	16
Canoeing	2	3	3	16
Sailing	2	3	3	11
Mountain climbing	1	1	--	--
Visiting zoos, amusement parks	--	--	24	73
Off-road driving	--	--	7	26
Other activities	5	--	24	--

[a] Ferriss (1962)
[b] Bureau of Outdoor Recreation (1972)
[c] Bureau of Outdoor Recreation (1973)
[d] Heritage Conservation and Recreation Service (1979)
  -- Data not available

While the surveys reported in Table 2-1 indicate, at least on the surface, the outdoor recreation activities in which participation is most widely distributed, their usefulness in recreation planning has been severely limited by a number of conceptual and methodological problems. The first of these stems from consideration of these surveys, either explicitly or implicitly, as studies of demand for recreational activities (Knetsch 1969; Burdge and Hendee 1972). These surveys are measures of participation, not demand. They do not take into account existing recreation opportunities and their effect on participation rates. It is likely that high participation rates will correlate with abundant opportunities, especially when these opportunities are priced at nominal levels, as is traditional in the public sector. A number of writers (e.g. Chappelle 1973) have observed that treating participation surveys as measures of demand leads to a feedback model whereby supply of opportunity creates high participation rates which in turn encourage more supply, and so on. Indeed, the supply of recreation opportunities has been found to have statistically significant effects on participation rates in at least two empirically-based studies (Cicchetti et al. 1969; Beaman et al. 1979).

Another conceptual problem with participation surveys is their exclusive focus on activities rather than the underlying meanings these activities have for participants. Recent theoretical and empirical work has shown that people participate in outdoor recreation activities to satisfy certain needs or motivations; recreation activities are more a means to an end than an end in themselves. Overemphasis on activities ignores the potential for one activity to substitute for another in fulfilling the same needs or motivations. The issues of motivations for recreation and substitutability are discussed in detail in Chapter Six.

Finally, participation surveys have been plagued by a host of methodological problems. The empty cells in Table 2-1 illustrate one such problem: the same activities are not always included in participation surveys, even when they are conducted under the auspices of the same agency. This lack of consistency limits comparisons over time and the identification of trends. Not apparent from Table 2-1, however, are other methodological inconsistencies. The way in which activities are defined can substantially affect the participation rates reported. The distinction between walking and hiking, for example, is often unclear, sometimes being left to the discretion of the respondent. The time period covered by the survey can also be a source of bias in participation surveys. Some surveys cover an entire calendar year while others focus on a single season. Other methodological issues include varying data collection techniques (e.g. personal, telephone, or mail surveys), sample size and response rate, age of respondents, recall period, and question wording and sequence.

Two studies in particular illustrate these methodological problems. Bevins and Wilcox (1979) examined 22 national outdoor recreation participation studies conducted between 1959 and 1978, including those in Table 2-1 along with several U.S. Forest Service camping market surveys, U.S. Fish and Wildlife Service surveys of hunting and fishing, and a number of market surveys conducted by private organizations. Data on 28 activities were explored, revealing some trends and a number of methodological problems. For example, participation in bicycling was included in thirteen surveys, but the range in nationwide participation varies from a low of 9 percent to a high of 47 percent, and no clear trend emerges from the data. Results for camping and hunting are somewhat more consistent, but there is still considerable variation between studies. It is usually impossible to distinguish which differences are caused by varying survey methods and which reflect real trends. In a similar comparative study, Stynes et al. (1980) conclude that examination of nationwide outdoor recreation participation surveys "may tell us more about the effects of alternative survey designs than about trends in participation."

More recently, use measurement research has focused on the distribution of outdoor recreation activity over both space and time. In an early study of the Boundary Waters Canoe Area, Minnesota, Lucas (1964a) mapped the spatial distribution of use and noted a highly uneven pattern of use. Over half of all types of visitors were found to use only one tenth of the access points to the study area. All studies examining the spatial distribution of use have documented similarly uneven patterns; most have focused on wilderness or related areas (Stankey et al. 1976; Leonard et al. 1978; Plumley et al. 1978; Lime 1977; Lucas 1980).

To quantify spatial distribution patterns more closely, a concentration index has been developed which relates amount of use to available area. The concentration index for the trial system of the Spanish Peaks Primitive Area, Montana, is shown in Figure 2-2. To compute the concentration index, trail segments are ranked by amount of use and use is summed and graphed, starting with the trail segments most used. The 45 degree diagonal represents perfectly evenly distributed use (i.e. 50 percent of all trail miles account for 50 percent of use), while the curved line plots the actual distribution of use. In Figure 2-2, 50 percent of all trail miles account for approximately 80 percent of all use. The concentration index is calculated on the basis of area A as a proportion of area A + B. Index values range from 0 (perfectly even distribution) to 100 (perfectly uneven distribution). The concentration index for the Spanish Peaks Primitive Area is 53, indicating relatively uneven distribution of use. Concentration indexes for seven wilderness areas studied by Lucas (1980) ranged from 53 to 78.

Spatial distribution of use of developed recreation areas also tends to be highly uneven. Manning et al. (1984), for example, calculated occupancy rates for campsites in selected Vermont state park campgrounds. Occupancy rates for campsites within the same campground were found to vary dramatically, usually ranging from less than 10 percent to greater than 80 percent.

Visitor use has also been found to vary sharply between recreation areas (Stankey et al. 1976; Peterson 1981). Comparison of use among ten wilderness areas within the national forests, for example, found that visitor-days of use varied dramatically. Even when use was related to acreage, some areas received approximately 500 times as much use as others (Stankey et al. 1976).

A few studies have examined the distribution of recreation use over time. As with the spatial distribution of use described above, these studies have found highly uneven patterns of recreation use. Not surprisingly, Lucas (1980) found use of nine western wilderness areas to be heavily concentrated within the three summer months. Even within this summer period, the large majority

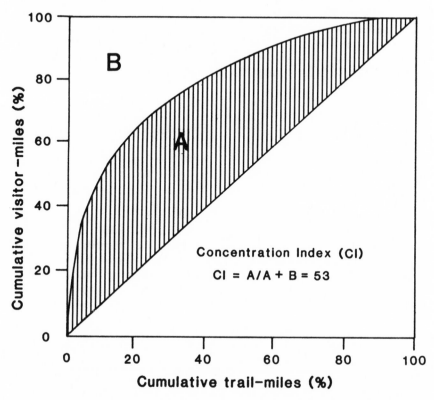

Figure 2-2. Spatial use concentration index for the trail system of the Spanish Peaks Primitive Area, Montana. (From Lucas 1980)

of visitors tended to enter the areas on weekends or holidays. Similar patterns of use have been found in more developed recreation areas (Hendee et al. 1976). Weekends and holidays accounted for the majority of all summer use in nearly all roaded areas studied within the national forests of Oregon and Washington. Manning and Cormier (1980) calculated use concentration indexes for the temporal distribution of use at state park campgrounds in Vermont and New Hampshire. Index values ranged from 12 to 45 indicating relatively uneven distribution of use over time.

Both spatial and temporal use of outdoor recreation areas tends to be distributed in a highly uneven fashion. This phenomenon creates several potential problems. Recreation facilities and services developed to meet peak loads are often largely unused at other times, resulting in inefficient resource use. In addition, the potential for crowding and conflicting uses is enhanced when a relatively large percentage of all visitors are concentrated in the same areas and/or time periods. And it may be that environmental impacts of recreation use are exacerbated by excessively concentrated patterns of use.

Social Correlates of Outdoor Recreation

From the amount and distribution of recreation activity, social scientists in outdoor recreation turned to the social characteristics of participants. This information is fundamental to an eventual understanding of more sophisticated issues such as why people participate in outdoor recreation, and is also important in predicting future recreation patterns and evaluating issues of social equity (Marcin and Lime 1977).

Research into the social characteristics of participants in general leisure activities began in the 1930s. These studies multiplied in the 1950s and 1960s when increased leisure became more generally available. Total participation in leisure activities, as well as in selected types of leisure activities, was generally found to be related to a variety of socio-economic factors, particularly social class differences and occupational prestige (e.g. MacDonald et al. 1949; Reissman 1954; White 1955; Thomas 1956; Clarke 1956; Havighurst and Feigenbaum 1959; Gerstl 1961; Dowell 1967; Bishop and Ikeda 1970). This body of literature has been summarized and interpreted particularly well by deGrazia (1962) and Cheek and Burch (1976).

Publication of the ORRRC reports in 1962 extended this work more directly to outdoor recreation. Two of the ORRRC studies in particular focused on social correlates of outdoor recreation participation. Sessoms (1961; 1963) reviewed 48 studies relating to this issue conducted between 1950 and 1962. Five socio-economic variables were found to be related to outdoor recreation patterns:

1. Age—The older one becomes, the fewer the recreation activities pursued and the more passive the activities.

2. Income—The higher one's income, the more numerous are the recreation activities pursued.

3. Occupation—The higher one's occupational prestige, the more numerous and varied are the recreation activities pursued.

4. Residence—Urban residents tend to have a higher participation rate in recreational activities than do rural residents.

5. Family stage—The presence of young children tends to reduce the number of recreation outings and makes the recreation pattern more home-centered.

This study was supplemented by an extensive nationwide household survey of outdoor recreation participation (Mueller and Gurin 1962). Participation in outdoor recreation activity was found to be "remarkably widespread," with about 90 percent of adults engaging in one or more activities in the course of a year. General participation was found to be statistically related to several socio-economic factors: age, race, region of residence, place of residence, education, income, and family life cycle. However, with the exception of age, relationships were only of weak to moderate strength, and all socio-economic variables combined explained only 30 percent of the variance in general outdoor recreation activity. Similar findings by Ferriss (1970) led to the conclusion that socio-economic characteristics "provide only a moderately satisfactory basis for predicting outdoor recreation participation."

Research conducted since the ORRRC studies has tended to corroborate these findings with some modifications. A number of studies conducted at various outdoor recreation sites are summarized in Table 2-2 to the degree they are comparable. They show a nearly uniform association of the use of outdoor recreation areas with certain income, education, occupation, and age characteristics. Younger persons of high socio-economic status predominate compared to their distribution throughout the general population, though they are, of course, not the only users of outdoor recreational areas.

While most of the recent data on social correlates of outdoor recreation have come from on-site studies, several household surveys have developed additional insights on this issue. Burdge (1969) surveyed residents of Allegheny County, Pennsylvania, as to their participation in selected leisure and outdoor recreation activities and their occupations. Occupational prestige was classified into four levels. Persons in the highest two occupational levels were found to have significantly higher participation rates in 13 of the 16 outdoor recreation activities studied. In addition, there is some evidence in Burdge's data that different types of outdoor recreation activities appeal to different occupational classes. Six recreation activities described by Burdge as potentially more expensive and less generally available were statistically related to the highest occupational prestige level, while four activities deemed more generally available were statistically related to the second highest occupational level. Moreover, two of the three recreation activities which were unrelated to any occupational prestige level were likely the most generally available of all. These findings corroborate results of research into more general leisure activities. The leisure activities of reading and studying, for example, have been found to be positively related to occupational prestige while resting, relaxing, watching television, and working around the house are inversely related (Clarke 1956).

Preliminary evidence of similar differential relationships with regard to income and education has been reported by Lindsay and Ogle (1972). A household survey of urban residents living close to a national forest found no relationship between income level of respondents and participation in outdoor recreation in the study area, and an inverse relationship between education and participation. It has been suggested (Harry 1972) that these findings, which on the surface appear to contradict the bulk of the literature, may indicate that

Table 2-2. Selected socio-economic characteristics of outdoor recreationists.

Study	Area	Predominate characteristic of the sample population[a]			
		Income	Education	Occupation	Age
Wagar 1963	2 national forest recreation areas	Middle	Middle to high	—	Young to middle-aged adults
Etzkorn 1964	1 California campground	—	High	Professional/technical	—
Love 1964	12 national forest campgrounds	—	—	—	Children to young adults
Shafer 1965	4 state park campgrounds	Middle to high	—	—	—
King 1965; 1968	National forest campgrounds	Middle	High	Middle to high prestige levels	—
Burch and Wenger 1967	A variety of camping areas	High	High	White collar/skilled	—
Hendee et al. 1968	3 wilderness areas	—	High	—	Young to middle-aged adults
Boster et al. 1973	Colorado River, Grand Canyon	High	—	—	—
Murray 1974	Southern Appalachian Trail	High	High	Professional/technical and students	Teenage to young adults
Lee 1975	Yosemite National Park	—	High	Professional/technical	—
Vaux 1975	4 wilderness areas	High, except students	—	—	—
Echelberger and Moeller 1977	National forest backcountry	Middle to high	Middle to high	—	Young adults

Table 2-2. Selected socio-economic characteristics of outdoor recreationists. (Cont.)

| Study | Area | Predominate characteristic of the sample population[a] | | | | |
		Income	Education	Occupation	Age
Towler 1977	Grand Canyon National Park backcountry	High	High	Professionals/ students	Young adults
Stankey 1980a	2 wilderness areas	--	High	--	Young to middle-aged adults
Lucas 1980	9 wilderness areas	Middle to high	High	Professional/ technical and students	Young to middle-aged adults

[a] The socio-economic categories reported in this table are highly generalized to enable reasonable comparison between studies and over time.

-- Data not available.

such generally available outdoor recreation opportunities may simply not appeal to persons of higher socio-economic status.

A household survey of visits to national parks in the Pacific Northwest (Bultena and Field 1978) offers further insight into the relationship between income and outdoor recreation. The percentage of respondents who had visited one or more national parks rose progressively with increased socio-economic status. Socio-economic status was then broken into its three component variables (income, education, and occupation) and each was tested for its relationship to national park visits. To isolate each of these three variables, statistical controls were applied to the other two. While education and occupation retained their statistically significant relationship with national park visits, income did not.

Similar results have been suggested in the data of other studies. Mueller and Gurin's (1962) survey, described earlier, found a positive but curvilinear relationship between income and outdoor recreation participation; participation in outdoor recreation rose with income up to a certain level, then declined slightly. It appears that income is related to participation only as it limits opportunity. At an income level sufficient to ensure that most outdoor recreation opportunities are reasonably available, it becomes less important relative to other factors such as education and occupation. Lucas (1964a) has noted similar results, and suggests that income itself is actually not a causal factor in outdoor recreation activity but simply correlates with the education and occupation of participants. From his study of visitors to the Boundary Waters Canoe Area, Minnesota, he concludes:

> Income seems to be more *necessary* than *sufficient* as an explanation of recreation choices. Money does not form tastes, it limits their expression (Lucas 1964a, p. 46).

A large-scale study by Kelly (1980) has corroborated many of the findings described above, and placed them in a more comprehensive perspective. The study involved a secondary analysis of data derived from a nationwide survey of outdoor recreation participation (Heritage Conservation and Recreation Service 1979). The thirty outdoor recreation activities studied were divided into three groups: forest-based activities, water-based activities, and outdoor sports activities. Seven socio-economic characteristics of respondents (family life cycle, family income, sex, race, age, occupation, and education) explained less than 10 percent of the variance in participation in each of the three groups of activities. It seems clear that socio-economic variables are generally not powerful predictors of outdoor recreation participation. However, in a second phase of the study, Kelly tested a large number of relationships between selected socio-economic characteristics and individual outdoor recreation activities. As suggested above, socio-economic characteristics were found to have differential effects on participation according to the character of the recreation activity. For example, age is strongly and inversely related to activities requiring physical strength and endurance, and income is related to only a few activities that have high costs. These findings suggest it is not surprising that socio-economic variables do not explain much of the variance in overall outdoor recreation participation when examined in an aggregate or multivariate context.

Two important methodological issues have been raised with regard to many of the studies discussed in this section. First, Jubenville (1971) has noted that on-site studies often focus exclusively on the "leader" of a recreation party and suggests this approach may be a source of bias. A test of this hypothesis was conducted on the Anaconda-Pintlar Wilderness Area, Montana, by interviewing both party leaders and all party members over age 14. Statistically significant differences were found between the two samples with regard to five socio-economic variables. Party leaders were more likely to be males, to have higher income and educational levels, to be in professional and technical occupations, and to have more years of recreation experience. These findings have been generally replicated by Lucas and Oltman (1971).

Another issue of concern focuses on differences between on-site studies and more broadly based surveys of the general population. It was noted earlier in this section that Mueller and Gurin's (1962) nationwide household survey found that 30 percent of the variance in outdoor recreation activity could be explained by seven socio-economic variables. This study, by definition, included both participants and non-participants in outdoor recreation. Field and O'Leary (1973) also conducted a household survey, their study focusing on participation in selected water-based recreation activities in the Pacific Northwest. When non-participants were excluded from the analysis, however, a group of seven of the most important socio-economic variables explained less than 12 percent of the variance in participation among the four water-based activities studied. The implication of this finding seems to be that much of the variation in socio-economic characteristics found in household surveys is a function of distinctions between outdoor recreation participants and non-participants. When non-participants are eliminated (as they are by definition in on-site studies), the resulting populations are substantially more homogeneous, at least with respect to traditional socio-economic measures.

Two other household surveys (O'Leary and Pate 1979; O'Leary and Weeks 1979) have generally corroborated the above findings. The former study found virtually no differences in socio-economic characteristics between participants in selected water-based recreation activities (examined by type of facility used and rate of participation). The latter study found relatively few significant differences in socio-economic characteristics between recreationists involved in consumptive (e.g. hunting and fishing) and appreciative (e.g. wildlife observation and hiking) outdoor recreation activities. Finally, an on-site study by Echelberger et al. (1974) in Tuckerman Ravine, New Hampshire, found no differences in socio-economic characteristics between skiers and hikers. The two groups, however, were found to have substantial differences of opinion with regard to management; skiers were more concerned with increasing the comfort and convenience level of the area, for example, while hikers were more concerned with the large number of people using the area.

The broader implication of these findings is that on-site studies of recreation visitors sample a relatively limited diversity of the general population, at least as defined by socio-economic characteristics. More broadly based studies of the general population may be needed to assess satisfaction and other aspects of outdoor recreation opportunities on a more comprehensive basis.

Cultural Influences on Outdoor Recreation

The studies described in the preceding section have isolated a number of social correlates of outdoor recreation. However, the relationships are generally of moderate strength at best and fail to explain a large percentage of the variation in outdoor recreation participation. Burdge and Field (1972) describe the results of this early period of research as "both productive and disappointing" and go on to suggest an alternative perspective for outdoor recreation research. They point out that a basic tenet of the social sciences is that human behavior is culturally influenced, and suggest that studies of outdoor recreation behavior include a component focusing on the cultural context of recreation participation.

Perhaps the earliest work in this area was that of Burch who theorized that outdoor recreation, like most other behavior, is largely a function of the groups in which one operates:

> The same individual who goes hunting with an all male group will behave differently than when he is taking his family fishing. Furthermore, these two groups will have different auxiliary activities and make different demands on the resource and recreation facilities. In other words, there is something in the nature of a recreation group which structures the group member's behavior (Burch 1964, p. 708).

Using primarily observational techniques, he found preliminary empirical support for the notion that recreation activities are often characterized by the group structure of their participants, with different groups having unique objectives and needs. Further theoretical development led to a "personal community hypothesis" of recreation: that participation in recreation is influenced by one's "social circles of workmates, family and friends" (Burch 1969). Again, preliminary empirical evidence from a study of camping tended to support this notion.

Consideration of the cultural influences on recreation has expanded considerably since the early 1970s, concentrating primarily on social groups. Meyersohn (1969) pointed out in his early review of the sociology of leisure that most social research in recreation has been based on random samples of individuals whereby the "connectedness of humans is carefully sampled out." Cheek (1971) demonstrated the potential shortcoming of this traditional approach by noting the prevalence of social groups in outdoor recreation. This study of visits to local parks by adult males found the vast majority (81 percent) came in social groups rather than alone. This finding has been consistently corroborated for most outdoor recreation areas and activities. The dominance of social groups in outdoor recreation environments is suggestive of the influence of group context on recreation behavior (Cheek and Burch 1976; Cheek et al. 1976). Empirical tests have consistently borne out this influence.

Field and associates (Field and O'Leary 1973; Field and Cheek 1974), for instance, studied participation in four water-based recreation activities using both conventional socio-economic variables and a measure of social groups (classified as family, friends, or family and friends). Examined independently, none of the nine socio-economic variables studied accounted for significant differences in participation rates in two of the four activities studied; for the third activity, only one variable was related to participation rates. Examined in a multivariate context, the nine socio-economic variables explained less than 5 percent of the variance in the three activities and 26 percent in the fourth. When type of social group was analyzed, however, significant differences were found in participation rates. Moreover, when the measure of social group was added to the nine socio-economic variables in a multivariate analysis, the amount of variance explained in participation rose to between 12 and 39 percent for the four activities.

Dottavio et al. (1980) also studied social groups in conjunction with socio-economic variables. Using a state-wide sample of Indiana residents, participation rates in twelve outdoor recreation activities were related to two independent variable sets: seven conventional socio-economic variables, and social group (measured as alone, family, friends, family/friends) combined with age and sex of respondent. The second set of variables explained substantially more variance in absolute frequency of participation than the first. It should be noted, however, that when the dependent varible of participation rate was dichotomized into high/low participation, the difference between the two independent variable sets was greatly reduced.

While the above studies indicate that social groups influence recreation participation, there is little to suggest why such influences exist. Buchanan et al. (1981) attempted to illuminate this issue by studying both social group influences on and motivations for recreation participation.[2] Using a sample of visitors to a multiple-use reservoir, social group (defined as family, friendship, and family/friendship) was related to participation in three water-based activities and nineteen potential recreation motivations were rated by respondents. Results indicated that social groups varied in the frequency with which they participated in the three activities studied. Moreover, this variability appeared to be related to the different motivations associated with these activities. The activity most heavily predominated by one social group also had the least variability in motivations assigned to it. On the other hand, the activity with

---

[2] The subject of motivations for recreation is addressed in detail in Chapter Six.

the greatest mix of social groups participating had the greatest variability in motivations. These findings may indicate that social groups are attracted to recreation activities based on motivations inherent within the group.

While the predominant focus of research into cultural influences on outdoor recreation has been social groups, several other variables have received limited attention. These include childhood experiences as part of the socialization process, effects of community type, and status group dynamics.

Several studies have examined childhood influences on outdoor recreation behavior in later life, all finding significant effects. Burch and Wenger (1967) studied childhood experience with nature and its relationship to style of camping selected as an adult: easy access camping, remote camping, or a combination of the two. Both those who had childhood hiking experience and—perhaps more surprisingly—those who had participated in auto camping as children were more likely to practice remote or combination camping than easy access camping. Easy access campers were more likely to be people without either hiking or auto camping experience as children. The authors conclude:

> . . . activities pleasantly familiar to a person in his childhood tend to attract his leisure-time interest as an adult. Furthermore, an adult with previous familiarity with the out-of-doors apparently prefers more challenging camping experiences, at least part of the time, than does the person new to the out-of-doors (Burch and Wenger 1967, p. 18).

The importance of childhood experiences was corroborated by Christensen and Yoesting (1973) in a household survey of recreation participation. The total number of recreation activities participated in as a child was combined with seven other independent variables (most conventional socio-economic and demographic measures) to explain 46 percent of the variance in adult recreation participation. Moreover, total childhood recreation activities were more important in explaining this variance than all the socio-economic and demographic variables combined. Yoesting and Christensen (1978) later replicated their study, obtaining very similar results: 36 percent of the variance in adult recreation activities was explained by the number of recreation activities participated in as a child. The authors point out, however, that participation in specific activities does not carry over from childhood as well as the general level of activity, and that socialization in recreation is apparently a lifelong process, influenced by a number of variables including social group. Sofranko and Nolan (1972), Yoesting and Burkhead (1973), and Kelly (1974) have also corroborated the importance of childhood activities to adult recreation participation.

Type of community has also been found to exert an influence on recreation behavior. The studies described in the preceding section of this chapter demonstrated relationships between various socio-economic characteristics of the individual and recreation participation. But Bultena and Field (1980) found these relationships to be mitigated by the social-class structure of the community in which the individual resides. Household samples were drawn from two communities varying distinctly in social-class structure—one a predominantly middle-class community, the other a predominately working-class community. Visitation rates to national parks were studied in both communities. Working-class people in the predominantly middle-class community were found to visit the parks significantly more frequently than their class counterparts in the predominantly working-class community. Conversely, park visitation rates of middle-class people in the working-class community were lower than their class counterparts in the middle-class community.

The theory of status group dynamics has also received empirical attention as a cultural influence on recreation. This theory suggests that participation in recreation, particularly faddish activities, is diffused through the population on a social class basis. The theory is based on the classic work of Veblen (1912) who observed that upper-class styles of leisure, as well as more general taste and consumption behavior, are often emulated and adopted by those of lower classes as a means of status mobility. West (1977; 1982a; 1983; 1984) has operationalized and tested this theory finding it useful in predicting and explaining outdoor recreation participation patterns. He found a number of outdoor recreation activities, such as bicycling, canoeing, and cross-country skiing, to be diffused over time from higher to lower social groups.

The studies examined in this section demonstrate that recreation behavior, particularly participation in recreation activities, can be more fully understood through consideration of the cultural context in which individuals operate. This is in keeping with the views developed in the broader social science disciplines that human behavior is, in large part, culturally determined.

Summary and Conclusions

1. *Information on recreation use and users has many potential applications to management. This type of information should be collected on a regular basis to document trends in recreation use patterns.*

2. *The first and simplest form of research on social aspects of outdoor recreation was on-site use measurement. Though relatively long historical records of use are available for some areas and agencies, application and meaning of these data are limited by lack of standardization in measurement units and methods.*

3. *General population studies in the form of participation surveys have also been used to measure outdoor recreation activity. However, the application and meaning of these data have also been limited by the confounding effects of supply on participation, emphasis on activities rather than underlying meanings, and a number of methodological inconsistencies.*

4. *Use of outdoor recreation areas tends to be distributed in a highly uneven fashion over both space and time. This pattern of use has resulted in inefficiencies of resource use and has exacerbated problems of crowding and environmental impacts.*

5. *People with diverse socio-economic characteristics participate in outdoor recreation. However, participants in some activities can be characterized by their relatively young age and high socio-economic status. However, socio-economic variables are not powerful predictors of general outdoor recreation activity.*

6. *Cultural context also influences outdoor recreation participation and behavior. Important cultural influences include one's social group, childhood and other socialization experiences, the type of community in which one lives, and a general social class tendency toward status emulation.*

Chapter Three

Descriptive Aspects
of Outdoor Recreation:
Attitudes, Preferences, Perceptions

User Attitudes and Preferences

Along with outdoor recreation activity patterns and social and cultural influences on recreation participation, the attitudes and preferences of visitors were an early focus of research. Recognition of recreation as social activity led naturally to the notion that information on visitor attitudes and especially preferences for facilities and services would be desirable in formulating recreation policy. Research in this area was further stimulated by the suggestion, stemming primarily from the academic community, that the expectations of visitors may differ in substantive ways from the perceptions of managers. The earliest attitude and preference studies tended to focus on developed recreation areas—primarily automobile campgrounds—while most recent emphasis has been placed on backcountry or wilderness environments. A specialized issue within this general research area is perception by visitors of environmental impacts.

Developed Areas. Studies of attitudes and preferences of visitors to developed recreation areas have used two basic research approaches: 1) the direct question technique where recreationists are asked to state their opinions in either an open-ended or, more commonly, a structured format, and 2) observation of user behavior. In several cases, both approaches have been used simultaneously, providing insights into the validity of study findings.

Results of several studies which can be compared directly are summarized in Tables 3-1 and 3-2. Table 3-1 presents data on desirable characteristics of campsites. Most campers find partial shade to be desirable, strongly prefer flush toilets, prefer spacing between campsites in the 50 to 100 foot range, prefer to be located between 100 and 200 feet from both comfort station and drinking water supply, strongly prefer some vegetative screening between campsites, and favor fireplaces constructed of metal. Table 3-2 presents data on characteristics of campgrounds which contribute to or detract from their popularity. Nearness to water or other major tourist attraction was an important factor common to all the studies. The size of the campground (number of campsites) was found to be related to campground use in two studies, but in opposite directions.

Table 3-1. Visitor preferences for developed area campsite conditions.

Study	Area	Research approach	Shade[a]	Flush toilets[b]	Campsite spacing[a]	Distance to comfort station[a]	Distance to drinking water[a]	Screening between sites[b]	Type of fireplace[a]
Love 1964	12 national forest campgrounds	Observation	--	--	>100 ft.	--	<200 ft.	84%	--
Shafer and Burke 1965	4 Pennsylvania state parks	Survey	Partial	85%	50-100 ft.	--	--	--	--
Cordell and Sykes 1969	1 national forest campground	Survey	--	93%	Approx. 80 ft.	100-200 ft.	<100ft.	90%	Metal
James and Cordell 1970	1 national forest campground	Survey & observation	Partial	--	--	--	--	--	--
Cordell and James 1972	1 national forest campground	Survey & observation	Partial	--	Approx. 80 ft.	100-200 ft	<100 ft.	--	Metal
Knudson and Curry 1981	3 Indiana state parks	Survey	--	--	40-65 ft.	--	--	--	--

[a] Condition preferred by majority of respondents
[b] Percent of respondents preferring this condition
-- Data not available

Table 3-2. Campground characteristics related to developed campground use.[a]

Study	Campground characteristics	Relationship to campground use
Beardsley 1967 (21 national forest campgrounds)	Presence of a recreationally useable water body within ¼ mile	Positive
Shafer and Thompson 1968 (24 New York state parks)	Number of sites	Positive
	Location proximate to a major tourist attraction	Positive
Lucas 1970 (22 national forest campgrounds)	Number of sites	Negative
	Yards of beach	Positive
	Type of water located close by	In decreasing order of preference: canoeable rivers, lakes, large rivers, creeks
	Distance from Great Lakes	Negative
Lime 1971 (34 national forest campgrounds)	Percent of waterfront campsites	Positive
	Reputation for good fishing	Positive
	Length of time open	Positive

[a] All studies listed used the research approach of observation.

It should be noted, however, that while these studies generally report majority opinions, there is often much diversity in the data. Authors of these studies have usually been careful to point this out. Cordell and Sykes (1969), for example, state that their study findings "represent majority opinion, but there are many campers who would prefer something quite different." Lucas (1970) also suggests that because of diversity in preferences, "A standard pattern of development does not seem appropriate." Perhaps no study has emphasized and illustrated this issue as well as Shafer (1969) who developed the example of the "average camper who doesn't exist." He points out that statistical averages sometimes obscure real diversity and create a model of reality which no one actually fits. Aggregating such data, particularly when drawn from different campgrounds and different time periods, may be akin to trying to "mate widgeons and wombats" (Shafer 1969).

Another methodological issue concerns correspondence of findings from studies using survey and observational techniques.[1] Studies using both techniques simultaneously have met with mixed results. An early study of camping (James and Cordell 1970; Cordell and James 1972), for example, surveyed visitors to a campground asking about preferred campsite characteristics, while at the same time observing actual campsite selection patterns. The authors report "a comforting amount of parallelism" in the findings from both research approaches; campers tended to select campsites with the characteristics they said they preferred. Shafer (1969) also reported relatively good agreement between findings obtained through survey and observational techniques, as have Klukas and Duncan (1967). Lime (1971), however, obtained more varied findings. While both survey and observational techniques revealed the strong influence of water-orientation in campground selection, there was less agreement about the influence of other variables. Hancock (1973) also found differences between stated preferences and observed behavior of recreation visitors in a study which experimentally reduced vegetative screening and groundcover at campsites. When surveyed, campers stated their nearly unanimous preference for existing conditions, but observation showed that occupancy rates of the study campsites increased after screening had been thinned. The survey technique seems most appropriate for the study of variables of which respondents are consciously aware, such as water-orientation, and for questions which are not hypothetical and those where there is little reason to expect bias. The most valid approach is to rely on a balance between research techniques, each acting as a check on validity for the other.

Finally, it should be noted that all of the studies reported are highly site-specific and the degree to which their findings can be generalized to other facilities and areas may be limited. There is considerable evidence in these studies that visitors tend to respond favorably to the facilities they find. This is reflected in the generally high levels of satisfaction reported by visitors over the variety of conditions found within the study areas. The reason for this is not clear. Visitors may sort themselves among facilities and areas according to their preferences, or their preferences might be based largely on the type of facilities and areas previously encountered. A study of river recreationists (McCool and Utter 1981), for example, found that preferences for management actions were diverse, but that they seemed to be associated with management systems under which respondents had previously operated. Unless preferences are found to be relatively consistent over a variety of facilities and areas, it would be unwise to generalize findings from this type of research.

---

[1] This issue is discussed in additional detail in Chapter Five.

Backcountry Areas. Results of several studies of backcountry visitor attitudes and preferences which are directly comparable are summarized in Tables 3-3 and 3-4. Studies of backcountry visitor attitudes toward management policies (Table 3-3) indicate that:

1. Most visitors favor use limitations. It should be noted, however, that the general form of this question is posed in terms of whether use limits would be favored or opposed if the study area were "overused."

2. There is no consensus on the method by which use limits should be administered. A lottery appears to be the least favored alternative.

3. Fixed travel routes or itineraries appear to be very unpopular.

4. A majority of visitors support self-registration.

5. Reaction is mixed on zoning by method of travel, lowering trail standards, and restricting or downgrading access routes.

6. Most visitors favor limits on party size.

7. Reaction is mixed on prohibition of campfires.

8. Most visitors favor use of helicopters for both administration and emergency use.

9. Most visitors favor fish stocking in wilderness areas.

Studies of backcountry visitor preferences for facilities and services (Table 3-4) indicate that:

1. Relatively low standard trails are preferred to high standard trails.

2. Most visitors prefer to find bridges at large streams which might be difficult or dangerous to ford.

3. Information signs (e.g. trail names, directions, and distances) are favored along trail systems, while campsite and interpretive signs are generally not favored.

4. Fireplaces and picnic tables are generally not preferred at campsites, while firerings are.

5. Opinion is mixed on pit toilets and other types of sanitary facilities at campsites.

6. Opinion is mixed on trail shelters.

7. Special facilities for horse use such as corrals and hitching racks are generally not favored.

8. Emergency telephones are generally not favored.

9. The majority of visitors prefer to have maps and informational pamphlets available.

10. The majority of visitors favor the presence of wilderness rangers.

All of the above studies have relied on survey techniques as the basic research approach, since observational techniques are difficult in backcountry environments where use is generally light and widely dispersed. A few studies of backcountry visitor preferences, however, have used observational techniques.

Text continues on page 36

Table 3-3. Visitor attitudes toward selected backcountry management policies.

Study		Percent favoring							
			Rationing system						
		Use limits	First-come first-served	Reser-vation	Lottery	Merit	Entrance fee	Fixed itinerary	Reg trati
Stankey 1973		--	28	18	48	--	23	8	--
Lucas 1980		--	--	--	--	--	--	--	**
Stankey 1980	A	76	41	29	18	--	--	25	23
	B	92	57	59	11	57	30	17	--
Hendee et al. 1968		50	--	--	--	--	40	--	--
Echelberger and Moeller 1977		--	--	--	--	--	15	--	54
Bultena et al. 1981a		85	82	37	6	26	11	--	--
Towler 1977		**	--	--	--	--	*	--	--
Shelby et al. 1982	A	--	25	95	50	37	66	--	--
	B	--	50	73	28	42	66	--	--
	C	--	51	74	30	49	55	--	--
Utter et al. 1981		--	--	**	**	**	--	--	--
Echelberger et al. 1974		--	--	--	--	*	--	--	--

Types of users and locations of studies are as follows: Stankey 1973—hikers, horseback riders, canoeists, motorboaters in four wilderness areas; Lucas 1980—hikers and horseback riders in nine wilderness a Stankey 1980—*A*: hikers and horseback riders in Spanish Peaks Primitive Area, MT; *B*: hikers in Desola Wilderness Area, CA; Hendee et al. 1968—hikers and horseback riders in three wilderness areas; Echelbe and Moeller 1977—hikers in Cranberry Backcountry, WV; Bultena et al. 1981a—hikers in Mt. McKi National Park, AK; Towler 1977—hikers in Grand Canyon National Park, AZ; Shelby et al. 1982—*A*: flo on the Snake River, ID and OR; *B*: backpackers in Eagle Cap Wilderness, OR; C: backpackers in Mt. Jeffe Wilderness, OR; Utter et al. 1981—floaters on the Salmon River, ID; Echelberger et al. 1974—hikers and s in Tuckerman Ravine, NH.

Table 3-3. Visitor attitudes toward selected backcountry management policies. (Cont.)

						Helicopters	
	Zoning by method of travel	Lower trail stardards	Restrict access	Limit party size	Prohibition of fires		
ɪdy						admin.	emergency
ankey 1973	47	41	--	***	--	--	--
cas 1980	--	--	--	--	*	--	--
ankey A ɜ0	--	50	45	51	--	--	--
B	--	43	53	81	--	--	--
ndee et al. ɨ8	--	--	--	--	--	60	99
ɪelberger d Moeller ɪ7	--	--	--	--	--	--	--
ɪtena et al. ɜ1a	--	--	--	--	75	--	--
ʌler 1977	--	--	--	**	--	--	--
ɛlby A ɪl. ɨ2	--	--	--	--	--	--	--
B	--	--	--	--	--	--	--
C	--	--	--	--	--	--	--
ɛer et al. ɪ1	--	--	--	--	--	--	--
ɪelberger ɪ. 1974	--	--	--	--	--	--	--

ata not available

Mixed responses

Minority

Majority

Table 3-4.   Visitor preferences for backcountry facilities and services.

Study		High standard trails	Low standard trails	Bridges across large rivers	Information signs	Campsite signs	Interpretive signs	Fireplaces	Firerin
Stankey 1973	A	37	--	--	--	--	--	--	--
	B	35	--	67	--	52	--	--	--
	C	31	--	65	--	30	--	--	--
	D	35	--	62	--	26	--	--	--
Lucas 1980		*	**	**	**	--	--	***	**
Wildland Research Center 1962	A	--	--	--	--	--	--	--	--
	B	--	--	--	--	--	--	--	--
	C	--	--	--	--	--	--	--	--
Merriam and Ammmons 1968	A	25	--	--	90	--	--	34	--
	B	32	--	--	62	--	--	24	--
	C	10	--	--	67	--	--	52	--
Hendee et al. 1968		*	--	--	**	--	*	25	--
Echelberger and Moeller 1977		--	--	--	--	--	50	--	--
Murray 1974		--	**	--	--	--	--	--	--
Plumley et al. 1978		--	--	--	--	--	--	--	--

Types of users and location of studies are as follows: Stankey 1973—hikers, horseback riders, canoeists, motorboaters in A: Boundary Waters Canoe Area, MN; B: Bob Marshall Wilderness Area, MT; C: Bri Wilderness Area, WY; D: High Uintas Primitive Area, UT; Lucas 1980—hikers and horseback riders in wilderness areas; Wildland Research Center 1962—users in A: Mt. Marcy, NY; B: Boundary Waters Ca Area, MN; C: the High Sierras, CA; Merriam and Ammons 1968—hikers and horseback riders in A: Marshall Wilderness Area, MT; B: Mission Mountains Primitive Area, MT; C: Glacier National Park, Hendee et al. 1968—hikers and horseback riders in three wilderness areas; Echelberger and Moeller 19 hikers in Cranberry Backcountry, WV; Murray 1974—hikers on the Appalachian Trail; Plumley et al. 19 hikers on the Appalachian Trail.

Table 3-4. Visitor preferences for backcountry facilities and services. (Cont.)

ly		Picnic tables	Pit toilets, sanitary facilities	Trail shelters	Corrals	Hitching racks	Emergency telephones	Maps/pamphlets	Wilderness rangers
					Percent favoring				
key	A	--	63	--	--	--	--	60	70
	B	--	43	--	25	26	--	52	58
	C	--	22	--	4	4	--	60	68
	D	--	25	--	11	16	--	55	67
as 1980		*	*	--	***	--	--	**	**
dland earch ter	A	--	70	--	--	--	50	--	--
	B	--	50	--	--	--	26	--	--
	C	--	36	--	--	--	45	--	--
riam	A	34	--	15	--	--	62	--	--
mons	B	24	--	34	--	--	32	--	--
	C	52	--	76	--	--	12	--	--
dee et al.		40	--	60	20	--	--	**	--
elberger Moeller		--	--	35	--	--	--	--	63
rray 1974		--	--	--	--	--	--	--	--
nley et al.		--	--	49	--	--	--	--	--

ata not available
Minority
Majority
Mixed responses

Pfister (1977) observed campsite choice behavior of floaters on the Rogue River, Oregon, and related it to campsite characteristics. Heberlein and Dunwiddie (1979) observed campsite choice behavior of visitors to the Bridger Wilderness Area, Wyoming. One of the most important findings of this study was that visitors tended to camp at previously used sites rather than seeking out and establishing new sites. This finding has been corroborated in the Great Gulf Wilderness Area, New Hampshire (Canon et al. 1979), and the Eagle Cap Wilderness, Oregon (Cole 1982).

Unfortunately, no studies of backcountry visitor attitudes and preferences have employed both survey and observational methods, nor are the few observational studies directly comparable to any of the survey-based studies. Thus, little is known about the validity of either type of study.

As with the studies of developed recreation areas, caution must be used in interpreting the findings of the above studies and incorporating them into management policy. The data are generally averages which tend to obscure the characteristic diversity. Moreover, a number of studies have shown substantive differences of opinion among visitors depending upon characteristics such as mode of travel (Stankey 1973; Lucas 1980), whether or not they are participating in a commercial trip (Utter et al. 1981; Shelby et al. 1982), the extent to which visitor attitudes conform to institutional definitions of wilderness (Hendee et al. 1968; Stankey 1972; Tarbet et al. 1977; Schreyer and Roggenbuck 1981), and backcountry experience (Towler 1977; Vaske et al. 1980; Hammitt and McDonald 1983).

Furthermore, the data on backcountry areas, like the studies of developed areas, are site-specific. There is often diversity of opinion between visitors to different backcountry areas, which tends to limit the degree to which the data are generalizable to other areas. In addition, many of the findings from the above studies, and others which have not been reported, are subject to such widely varying methods of investigation (e.g., question wording and sampling procedures) that they are not directly comparable. Thus, they have little application beyond the study area.

Perceptions of Environmental Impacts

A small group of studies has focused on the perceptions of visitors of environmental impacts, particularly those caused by recreation use. A recent review of this issue has found the literature in this area to be rather sparse but generally indicative that visitors' perceptions of recreational impacts are limited (Lucas 1979). With the exception of litter, visitors rarely complain about site conditions and usually rate the environmental conditions of recreation sites as good or better. This appears true for impacts on campsites and trails, as well as other resource impacts such as water pollution and wildlife disturbance. Merriam and Smith (1974), for example, found that campers in the Boundary Waters Canoe Area, Minnesota, seldom commented on campsite impacts other than litter and that there was no correlation between visitor ratings of campsite physical condition and expert ratings of the severity of environmental impacts. Helgath (1975) found the vast majority of hikers in the Selway-Bitterroot Wilderness Area, Idaho and Montana, well-satisfied with trail conditions despite the fact that some trail areas were severely eroded. Solomon and Hansen (1972) report that only 1 percent of floaters on the Pine River in the Manistee National Forest, Michigan, were concerned with streambank erosion (which was very prominent), while 4 percent listed viewing and enjoying eroded banks as the high point of their trip. Litter was far and away the most objectionable environmental condition reported by users. The only impact reported by over 50 percent of visitors to roaded forest lands in the Pacific Northwest was litter (Downing and Clark 1979). Finally, only one in four campers viewed vegetation impacts as a problem at four heavily used developed campgrounds in Pennsylvania (Moeller et al. 1974).

Two more recent studies corroborate these findings. Knudson and Curry (1981) studied visitor perception of environmental impact at three Indiana state park campgrounds which were subject to varying levels of impact. The majority of campers rated ground cover conditions as satisfactory to excellent, even in areas where over three-fourths of the campsites were 100 percent bare or disturbed. Even the minority of respondents who rated ground cover poor or below reported that these conditions did not affect their enjoyment of the area. Moreover, two-thirds of respondents did not notice damage to trees or shrubs even though such damage was actually extensive in several areas. Hammitt and McDonald (1983) surveyed floaters on several southeastern rivers as to their experience with river floating and their perception of five environmental impacts. Experience was positively related to perception of impacts, but a large majority of floaters, even those classified as having high experience, failed to notice or report any of the five impacts studied.

Visitor Versus Manager Perceptions

At the beginning of this chapter it was suggested that objective information on outdoor recreation is needed because perceptions of recreation managers may differ from those of visitors. Studies on this issue have addressed three broad aspects of recreation: the meanings or motivations associated with recreation areas or activities, perceptions of recreation impacts and problems, and recreation area management.

Several studies have found rather consistent differences between visitors and managers with regard to the meanings of outdoor recreation. Two of the earliest studies illustrate these findings. Clark et al. (1971) surveyed visitors and managers of selected developed campgrounds in Washington State. Visitors generally reported high ratings on a number of the more traditional camping values such as experiencing "solitude and tranquility" and appreciating "unspoiled beauty." Managers substantially underestimated the importance of such values to campers, apparently unable to rationalize these values with use of developed campgrounds. The apparent incongruity of visitor values is evident in response patterns to two motivation items in particular. Nearly two-thirds of visitors rated "solitude and tranquility" as very important, while only about one-quarter rated "getting away from people other than my camping party" as very important. Apparently, solitude and tranquility are relative values and are defined by visitors to developed campgrounds somewhat differently than their conventional meanings in outdoor recreation.[2] These changing values are apparently not well understood by managers. In a similar study of Minnesota state parks, Merriam et al. (1972) found that users defined these areas primarily in terms of recreation, while managers defined them in terms of natural areas designed for preservation. A third study of this issue focused on an urban landscape resource: the University of Washington Arboretum (Twight and Catton 1975). Visitors were found to be more oriented to preservation and naturalness of the area than managers and less oriented to scientific, educational, and horticultural aspects. In all three studies, visitors define the study areas primarily in terms of what they use them for rather than the purposes for which the areas may have originally been established.

Two more recent studies have added additional insight to this issue. Wellman et al. (1982) explored how well managers were able to predict the motivations of visitors to two national park areas: Cape Hatteras National Seashore (a recreation area with substantial off-road vehicle use), and Shenandoah National Park backcountry (a natural area). Statistically significant differences were found between visitor and manager ratings on sixteen of 22 motivation items at Cape Hatteras and eight of 25 motivation items at Shenandoah. The authors suggest that the greater convergence of visitor and manager perceptions at Shenandoah might be explained by the fact that this area is more traditional in environment and use within the national park system than Cape Hatteras. Tentative support for this hypothesis is offered by a similar study of ski-touring on national forest lands in Colorado (Rosenthal and Driver 1983). Very close agreement was found in this study between visitor motivations and manager predictions. This study area was also primarily undeveloped backcountry more conventionally associated with outdoor recreation.

Four studies have included components which examine the different percep-tions of visitors and managers of recreation impact and problems. The findings have been highly consistent: managers are much more perceptive of such issues than visitors in all areas studied including developed campgrounds (Clark et al. 1971), wilderness (Peterson 1974), roaded forest lands (Downing and Clark 1979), and non-motorized recreation areas (Lucas 1979). Impacts and problems studied included litter, vandalism and theft, human waste, environmental impacts at campsites and along trails, water pollution, wildlife disturbance, excessive noise, rule violations, and conflicts between recreationists.

---

[2] This issue is discussed in more detail in Chapter Five.

The third broad aspect of recreation investigated by this group of studies is attitudes and preferences for area management. The first of these studies focused on visitors and managers of three western wilderness areas (Hendee and Harris 1970). Visitors were asked to rate the extent to which they agreed with an extensive list of wilderness attitude statements, policy and management alternatives, and appropriate behavior items. Wilderness managers were asked to predict visitor responses. Broad agreement was found on two-thirds of the items, but disagreement on the remaining items illustrated several important misconceptions of managers. Managers overestimated visitor support for facility development and the prevalence of "purist" attitudes (e.g., many visitors did not object to use of helicopters for management purposes though managers thought they would). Managers also anticipated strong opinions from visitors who were actually neutral or had no opinion on management issues. Lastly, managers underestimated the responsiveness of visitors to measures of behavioral control (e.g., camp clean-up requirements and restrictions on trail shortcutting). Differences in area management preferences between visitors and managers were also found by Clark et al. (1971), though they are not consistent with the results of the last study since they report that managers overestimated visitor opposition to increased area development. However, the differences in study areas may explain the apparent inconsistency of these two studies: the former was conducted in wilderness areas while the latter focused on developed campgrounds.

Nearly all the above studies have speculated on why differences in perception exist between managers and visitors. A popular theory suggests that managers are more oriented to the natural environment and traditional conceptions of outdoor recreation by virtue of their professional training in the natural sciences, especially biology, their rural residence, the professional missions under which they operate, and their experience with the natural environment, both generally and specifically on study sites. Another theory suggests a process of selective perception reinforcing the managers' attitudinal and perceptual predispositions. Inaccurate assessments of visitors may also result from the fact that managers most often come into contact with vocal and opinionated visitors who may not be representative of most visitors with more moderate or less-developed views. And, finally, managers' own attitudes may affect their perceptions of recreation visitors: a manager's opinion of what visitors *should* prefer may well influence his or her view of what visitors *do* prefer (Heberlein 1973). But regardless of the reason why, it is evident that managers and visitors of outdoor recreation areas often hold different perceptions. Neither can be considered "correct." But, as will be emphasized in later chapters, visitors are an important part of the outdoor recreation environment, and managers should seek out objective measures of visitor attitudes, preferences, and perceptions.

Summary and Conclusions

1. *Visitor attitude and preference studies have been conducted in a variety of developed and backcountry recreation areas. Findings from this type of study can be of considerable usefulness to planners and managers in meeting the needs and desires of visitors. However, caution must be used in interpreting such findings. Even though majority opinions are found on many factors, there is nearly always some diversity of opinion that should not go unheeded.*

2. *More observational studies are needed, especially in backcountry environments, as a check on validity of survey-based studies of visitor attitudes and preferences.*

3. *On-site studies of visitor attitudes and preferences tend to be highly site-specific, and results from these studies should be generalized to other areas only with considerable caution.*

4. *With the exception of litter, most visitors to outdoor recreation areas tend to have limited perception of environmental impacts caused by recreation use.*

5. *Managers' perceptions of visitors have been found inaccurate in several ways including the meanings or motivations associated with outdoor recreation, attitudes and preferences for management, and perceptions of recreation impacts and problems. These findings have reinforced the need for systematic and objective information about visitors.*

Chapter Four
Carrying Capacity: An Organizational Framework

Origins

Rapidly expanding recreation in the 1950s and 1960s gave rise to concerns over appropriate use levels of outdoor recreation areas. While interest in the impacts of recreation on the natural resource base predominated, there was also emerging attention on effects of increased use on the quality of the recreation experience. The early studies described in the preceding chapters prompted theorists to search for an organizational framework into which such data might be fit to help formulate outdoor recreation policy. The resulting paradigm was the concept of carrying capacity.

Carrying capacity has a rich history in the natural resource professions, substantially predating its serious adoption in the field of outdoor recreation. In particular, the term has received wide use in wildlife and range management where it refers to the number of animals of any one species that can be maintained in a given habitat (Dasmann 1964). But in its most generic form carrying capacity is a fundamental concept in natural resources and environmental management referring to the ultimate limits to growth of a dependent species as constrained by various natural factors of environmental resistance (Odum 1959). In this generic form carrying capacity has been applied to the most broad-ranging issues, including the ultimate population level of humans (Borgstrom 1965; Meadows et al. 1972) and general environmental planning (Godschalk and Parker 1975).

Perhaps the first suggestion for applying the concept of carrying capacity to outdoor recreation occurred in the mid-1930s. In his report on policy recommendations for parks in the California Sierras, National Park Service wildlife technician Lowell Sumner posed the question, "How large a crowd can be turned loose in a wilderness without destroying its essential qualities?" Later in his report he suggested that recreation use of wilderness be kept "within the carrying capacity" (Sumner 1936). A decade later Wagar (1946) wrote, "In all forest recreation, but particularly in zones of concentrated use, carrying capacity is important." With obvious links to the more traditional use of carrying capacity in wildlife biology, he went on to note, "We suspect that humans have saturation points akin to those shown by pheasants and quail." In a follow-up article, Wagar listed carrying capacity as one of eight major principles in recreation land use:

> Forestry, range management, and wildlife management are all based upon techniques for determining optimum use and limiting harvest beyond this point. Forest recreation belongs in the same category and will be more esteemed when so treated (Wagar 1951, p. 433).

The concept became a more formal part of the outdoor recreation field when determination of carrying capacity was listed as a major issue by Dana (1957) in his widely read problem analysis of outdoor recreation, and as a result of its prominence in the deliberations and writings of the Outdoor Recreation Resources Review Commission (ORRRC 1962).

Carrying Capacity and Recreation

The first rigorous application of carrying capacity to outdoor recreation came in the early 1960s with Wagar's (1964) conceptual monograph and a preliminary empirical treatment by Lucas (1964b). Perhaps the major contribution of Wagar's analysis was the expansion of carrying capacity from its dominant emphasis on environmental effects to a dual focus including social or experiential considerations:

> The study reported here was initiated with the view that the carrying capacity of recreation lands could be determined primarily in terms of ecology and the deterioration of areas. However, it soon became obvious that the resource-oriented point of view must be augmented by consideration of human values (Wagar 1964, preface).

Wagar's point was that as more people visit an outdoor recreation area, not only the environmental resources of the area are affected, but also the quality of the recreation experience. Thus carrying capacity was expanded to include consideration of the social environment as well as the physical/biological environment. The effects of increasing use on recreation quality were illustrated by Wagar by means of hypothetical relationships between increasing crowding and visitor satisfaction. Significantly, as will be discussed in following chapters, he suggested that the effects of crowding on satisfaction would vary, depending upon visitor needs or motivations.

Lucas (1964b) made a preliminary attempt to estimate the recreation carrying capacity of the Boundary Waters Canoe Area, Minnesota, and discovered that perceptions of crowding by different user groups varied. Paddling canoeists were found to be more sensitive to crowding than motor canoeists, who were in turn more sensitive to crowding than other motorboaters. A range of carrying capacities was estimated depending upon these different values.

Wagar (1964) hinted at a third concept inherent in carrying capacity in his original monograph and described it more explicitly in a later paper (Wagar 1968). Noting a number of misconceptions about carrying capacity, he pointed out that capacity might vary according to the amount and type of management activity. For example, the durability of environmental resources might be increased through practices such as fertilizing and irrigating vegetation, and periodic rest and rotation of impact sites. Similarly, the quality of the recreation experience might be maintained or even enhanced in the face of increasing use by means of more even distribution of visitors, appropriate rules and regulations, the provision of additional visitor facilities, and educational programs designed to encourage desirable user behavior. Thus carrying capacity, as applied to outdoor recreation, was expanded to a three-dimensional concept by the addition of management activity.

This three-dimensional view has been retained in contemporary analyses of carrying capacity, though it is sometimes described in terms of three types of carrying capacity. Alldredge (1973), for example, offers definitions for three kinds of recreation carrying capacity; resource-bearing, visitor, and facilities. Similarly, Heberlein (1977) discusses three types of capacity which he labels ecological, social, and facilities. A fourth type of capacity termed "physical" is also discussed by Heberlein, referring to the constraint imposed by sheer limits of physical space. This concept, however, is rarely of concern in management of outdoor recreation.

Change and Management Objectives

The early work of Wagar, Lucas, and others stimulated an intensive focus on carrying capacity as a research and management concept. Evidence of the extent of this interest is the annotated bibliography on recreational carrying capacity compiled by Stankey and Lime in 1973 which contained over 200 citations. But despite this impressive literature base efforts to apply carrying capacity to recreation areas often resulted in frustration. The principal difficulty lay in determining how much change should be allowed within each of the three components that make up the carrying capacity concept: the environmental resources, the quality of the recreation experience, and the extent and direction of management actions.

The growing research base on outdoor recreation indicated that increasing recreation use inevitably caused change. This was especially clear with regard to physical and biological resources. An early study in the Boundary Waters Canoe Area, for example, found that an average of 80 percent of ground cover vegetation was destroyed at campsites in a single season even under relatively light levels of use (Frissell and Duncan 1965). Deteriorating quality of the recreation experience as a function of increased use was generally assumed, though the empirical basis for such a relationship was limited. And experience had shown that increasing recreation use was met with more intensive management control. The critical question remained—how much change should be allowed?

Frissell and Stankey (1972) called this issue the "limits of acceptable change." Some change is inevitable, but sooner or later the amount, nature, or type of change becomes unacceptable. But what determines the limits of acceptable change? The answer given by most researchers is management objectives—indeed, no other theme has recurred so frequently in analyses of carrying capacity. Wagar (1964), in his original monograph, noted that, "there must be some management objective on which to base a satisfactory level of quality." More recent writers have emphasized the need for management objectives to be explicit and detailed. Frissell and Stankey, for instance, conclude:

> Unless the objectives are relatively clear, efforts to establish some "carrying capacity" will be futile. All too often objectives are either lacking, contradictory, or of such diffuse character that any effort to arrive at an estimation of capacity becomes impossible (Frissell and Stankey 1972, p. 180).

Likewise, Hendee et al. state:

> Only when . . . goals are reduced to specific area *management objectives*—formal statements of the environmental and social conditions that management seeks to maintain or to restore—can logical carrying capacity decisions be made. Statements of management objectives should thus be precise and site specific so they can serve as criteria for making carrying capacity decisions (Hendee at al. 1977, p. 172).

Numerous other reports also emphasize the need for management objectives (e.g., Lime and Stankey 1971; Lucas and Stankey 1974; Bury 1976; Brown 1977; Lime 1977a; Lime 1979; Stankey 1980b; Boteler 1984).

Management objectives provide an answer to the question of how much change is acceptable by deciding what type of recreational experience a particular recreation area should provide: the level of naturalness of environmental conditions, the kind of experience offered, and the intensity of management practices. These decisions constitute management objectives.

But how are such decisions made and management objectives formulated? The inescapable answer seems to be that they are value judgments. Research-based data can provide helpful inputs to such decisions. Research can help define the relationships between increasing recreation use and change in the recreation environment. But determining the point at which change becomes unacceptable is a value choice, not a technical issue. Recreation managers cannot avoid such value-laden judgments. Shelby and Heberlein (1984) illustrate the unavoidable element of value judgments in carrying capacity determinations. They describe two basic components of carrying capacity analysis: description and evaluation. The former documents observable relationships between recreation use and potentially important changes in the recreation environment such as environmental impacts and perceived crowding. The latter involves critical evaluation and judgment of the desirability of such changes. The authors propose the term "evaluative standards" rather than management objectives to emphasize the values inherent in such decisions.

Though determination of management objectives involves value judgments, it need not be arbitrary nor the exclusive province of managers. In fact, in today's climate of public involvement, such decisions *cannot* be arbitrary and stand the test of time. Neither can they only represent the values of managers themselves, for it was shown in the previous chapter that the perceptions of managers often differ in important ways from those of recreationists. Formulation of management objectives for outdoor recreation areas should be based on three broad considerations:

1. Natural Resource Conditions. The physical and biological characteristics of the natural resource base determine in large part the degree of change in the environment that results from recreation use. While even light levels of use will cause change in the environment, some resource bases are inherently more fragile than others. These resource characteristics should be studied and may become important constraints in formulating management objectives.

2. Institutional Factors. Legal directives and agency mission statements will often provide some guidance in determining appropriate resource, experience, and management conditions. The provisions of the Wilderness Act, for example, place considerable emphasis on naturalness of the environment and the experiential qualities of solitude and freedom. These directives should guide wilderness managers in setting objectives which emphasize relatively little change in the natural environment, low use density, and a relatively unrestrictive management approach.

3. Social Factors. The needs and wants of people are ultimately important in determining appropriate uses of natural resources. Without information on such needs and wants, management of natural resources for recreation is likely to be unfulfilling to both managers and users.

While the natural resource and institutional factors are critical in formulating management objectives, it is the social factors that are the focus of this study. Chapter Three has already examined studies of user attitudes and preferences and these findings can be important in formulating management objectives. Several other basic approaches have also been taken in defining these social factors; three of these, considered in later chapters, are 1) an empirical examination of the relationship between use density, perceived crowding, and recreation satisfaction, 2) the motivations for outdoor recreation, and 3) designs for diversity in outdoor recreation opportunities.

The Status of Carrying Capacity

Recreation carrying capacity has evolved from a simple suggestion to a rather complex concept involving resource, experience, and managerial considerations, an understanding of the role of change in the recreation environment, and the need for management objectives which involve difficult value judgments. Clearly there is no *one* carrying capacity for an outdoor recreation area. Rather carrying capacity is dependent upon how the various components of the concept are fashioned together. This complexity and apparent lack of definitiveness have caused considerable disillusionment. Characterizations of carrying capacity as "slippery" (Alldredge 1973), "elusive" (Graefe et al. 1984), and "illusive" (Becker et al. 1984) perhaps best describe the mood of current thinking. This difficulty with carrying capacity seems to be borne out in a recent survey of wilderness managers (Washburne 1981; Washburne and Cole 1983). Nearly half of the managers of designated wilderness felt they were unable to determine carrying capacities for any portion of their lands, even though two-thirds of them estimated that use exceeded capacity in at least part of their areas.

The weaknesses and shortcomings of carrying capacity have been noted by a number of writers. Several point out that the term implies a single magic number for each recreation area, and that this, of course, is misleading and obscures the role of value judgments (Bury 1976; Washburne 1982). For this reason, a stronger emphasis on management objectives has been suggested by some as an alternative to carrying capacity (Becker and Jubenville 1982; Jubenville and Becker 1983; Stankey et al. 1984). Similarly, Godin and Leonard (1977b) point out that analyses of carrying capacity often ignore the ability of management to affect use levels; they suggest the term "design capacity" would better reflect the proper role of management. Others have argued that the very term "carrying capacity" seems to imply an undue emphasis on use limitations (Washburne 1982; Stankey et al. 1984; Burch 1984). They argue that a number of management alternatives might be used to meet management objectives aside from use limitations, which may often be the least preferred alternative. Moreover, while management objectives for some areas may well set relatively low carrying capacities and thus ultimately require use limits, other areas will properly have relatively high capacities without need for use limits. In a similar vein, Stankey (1974) makes the important point that recreation-caused change is not inherently undesirable. In fact, he encourages use of the neutral word "change" as opposed to "damage" or other value-laden terms, since judgment about the relative desirability of change can only be made in relationship to management objectives. Finally, even Wagar (1974), author of the original monograph on recreation carrying capacity, has suggested that borrowing the concept from range and wildlife management may not have been a wise choice. The close association between carrying capacity and resource considerations in the historical sense tends to divert attention from the equally important experience and managerial concerns that must be a part of recreation carrying capacity.

All of these points are valid and have contributed to confusion over carrying capacity. But the term is deeply entrenched in the field of outdoor recreation and recent legislation and institutional directives have even made carrying capacity a formal part of recreation resource management. In the regulations implementing the National Forest Management Act of 1976, Section 219.18(a) states that the portion of forest plans providing direction for wilderness management will "provide for limiting and distributing visitor use of specific areas in accord with periodic estimates of the maximum levels of use that allow natural processes to operate freely and that do not impair the values for which wilderness areas were created." Amendments to Public Law 91-383 (84 Stat. 824, 1970) call for general management plans for units of the national park system to include "identification of and implementation commitments for visitor carrying capacities for all areas of the unit." Moreover, amendments to the National Trails System Act (Public Law 90-543, 1968) instruct the responsible secretary to develop a comprehensive plan for trails, including "an identified carrying capacity of the trail and a plan for its implementation." Finally, the Nationwide Outdoor Recreation Plan (Bureau of Outdoor Recreation 1973) states that "each federal recreation land managing agency will determine the carrying capacity of its recreation lands."

Despite its shortcomings, carrying capacity is likely to remain a part of the field for the foreseeable future and can be useful as an outdoor recreation management concept when viewed in proper perspective—as an organizational framework for the ideas discussed in this chapter.

Summary and Conclusions

1. *Since its adoption from wildlife and range management, outdoor recreation carrying capacity has evolved from a primary emphasis on natural resource impacts to include equal consideration of recreation experience and management considerations.*

2. *Recreation use inevitably results in change in the recreation environment: resource conditions, the experience provided, and/or management actions.*

3. *Limits must be placed on the amount of change acceptable.*

4. *The limits of acceptable change are value judgments which should be expressed in explicit and quantitative management objectives.*

5. *The value judgments inherent in management objectives should be based upon the broad considerations of resource conditions, institutional factors, and the needs and wants of society.*

6. *There is no single carrying capacity for an outdoor recreation area. Rather, every area has a range of capacities, depending upon the management objectives selected.*

7. *Carrying capacity does not necessarily imply strict limitation of use. Some recreation areas will have low capacities requiring use limits, while others will have high capacities with little need for use limits. Moreover, use limits are only one of several recreation management alternatives, and are often the least desirable.*

8. *Carrying capacity can be a useful outdoor recreation management concept when viewed as an organizational framework. In this respect, it is a means to an end rather than an end in itself.*

Chapter Five
Density, Crowding, and Satisfaction: Search For Relationships

Concern Over Crowding

This chapter examines a large and growing genre of research concerned with what is popularly called crowding in outdoor recreation. There is a relatively long history of concern over the effects of increasing use on the quality of the recreation experience, beginning even before the post-World War II boom in recreation participation (e.g., Adams 1930; Leopold 1934). Shortly after the beginning of the period of rapidly expanding outdoor recreation in the 1950s and 1960s a number of popular articles (e.g., DeVoto 1953; Clawson 1959) began to generate widespread interest in this topic.

Adoption of the concept of carrying capacity and particularly the expansion of the concept to include a social carrying capacity component provided a convenient foundation on which to base theoretical and empirical crowding research. Wagar's (1964) conceptual analysis of carrying capacity is again an appropriate place to begin discussion. Wagar suggested that, "When too many people use the same area, some traditional wildland values are lost," and he illustrated this suggestion with hypothetical relationships between crowding and satisfaction of a series of human needs inherent in outdoor recreation participation. Crowding was shown to have a detrimental effect on most of these values including a healthful environment, esteem and prestige, aesthetic enjoyment, understanding, freedom of choice, self-reliance, and solitude.

The notion that there is some level of visitor density beyond which the quality of the recreation experience diminishes is frequently repeated in the early outdoor recreation literature. This notion is at the heart of the social carrying capacity concept and has often contributed, along with concerns over environmental impacts, to regulation of the number of people using outdoor recreation areas. One of the earliest quantitative studies to indicate a social concern over crowding was conducted by the Outdoor Recreation Resources Review Commission (Department of Resource Development 1962). A large-scale survey of visitors at 24 outdoor recreation sites around the country found that nearly 20 percent of respondents said there were too many people using the area, though nearly an equal number felt they would have been satisfied with more people. Lucas (1964b) also found substantial concern over crowding among a sample of visitors to the Boundary Waters Canoe Area with 34 percent of paddling canoeists reporting being bothered "a little" or "quite a bit" by crowding. This declined to 16 percent and 8 percent of motor canoeists and motor boaters, respectively. In the campground environment, Lime (1971) found that nearly all campers sampled on the Superior National Forest, Michigan, preferred to be well separated from their neighbors. It should be noted that these expressions of concern, though representing a minority of users, were detected in early studies when use was low compared to use conditions of today.

Crowding in the wilderness environment has been studied extensively. Stankey (1973) asked visitors to four wilderness areas the extent to which they agreed with the statement: "It is reasonable to expect that one should be able to visit a wilderness area and see few, if any, people." In three wilderness areas in the west 77 percent of respondents were in agreement, while in the Boundary Waters Canoe Area 67 percent of respondents agreed. And in a series of studies in nine wilderness and related areas conducted from 1970 through 1972, Lucas (1980) reported a range of 13 percent to 49 percent of visitors who felt they met too many others during their trip.

Concern over crowding is apparently widely shared by managers of recreation areas as well as visitors. A recent survey of managers of wilderness and related areas (Washburne and Cole 1983) found that two-thirds of all areas were considered to be used beyond capacity in at least some places and at some times. In most of these cases (53 percent) the overuse problems were considered to be of a social or crowding nature as opposed to resource damage.

The Satisfaction Model

Early concerns over crowding were followed by theoretical development. Several theorists developed a quantitative model of the effects of increasing use on the recreation experience, based on the economic concept of marginal utility (Clawson and Knetch 1966; Fisher and Krutilla 1972; Alldredge 1973). Substituting recreation visits for input and satisfaction for output, the theoretical constructs of production economics suggest that as visitors are added to a recreation area the marginal satisfaction of each individual visitor will progressively decline due to crowding, but total or aggregate satisfaction will increase. This process continues until the marginal satisfaction of the nth visitor no longer exceeds the drop in satisfaction of previous visitors. At this point aggregate satisfaction begins to decline and social carrying capacity has been reached.

Alldredge (1973) illustrated the model with an example of a hypothetical wilderness area. Starting with the area devoid of visitors, no satisfaction is produced (see Table 5-1 and Figure 5-1).[1] As the first visitor enters the area he

---

[1] It is evident that wilderness and other outdoor recreation areas provide vicarious satisfaction and other values even when unvisited. The focus in this analysis, however, is on direct satisfaction derived by recreation visitors.

Table 5-1. Hypothetical relationship between increasing visitor use and satisfaction.

Number of visitors	Average satisfaction per visitor[a]	Total satisfaction	Marginal satisfaction
0	0	0	0
1	36	36	36
2	34	68	32
3	32	96	28
4	30	120	24
5	28	140	20
6	26	156	16
7	24	168	12
8	22	176	8
9	20	180	4
10	18	180	0
11	16	176	− 4
12	14	168	− 8
13	12	156	−12
14	10	140	−16
15	8	120	−20
16	6	96	−24
17	4	68	−28
18	2	36	−32
19	0	0	−36
20	−2	−40	−40
21	−4	−84	−44

Adapted from Alldredge (1973)

[a] Measured in hypothetical units of satisfaction which Alldredge terms "enjoyils."

or she experiences maximum satisfaction, arbitrarily defined as 36 units. As a second visitor is added, the satisfaction of the first visitor is reduced slightly due to very low level crowding and the satisfaction of the second visitor is also less than maximum. Even though average satisfaction falls with each additional visitor, total satisfaction continues to rise (though at a declining rate) while marginal satisfaction (the change in total satisfaction) is above zero. As the tenth visitor—in this example—is added, his or her satisfaction just equals the aggregate drop in satisfaction experienced by the other visitors and total satisfaction is at its highest. Social carrying capacity has been reached. This is the point at which marginal satisfaction equals zero.

The driving force behind this model is an assumed inverse relationship between use density and satisfaction; for the individual, increased density causes decreased satisfaction. This approach to crowding has been called the "satisfaction model" (Heberlein and Shelby 1977).

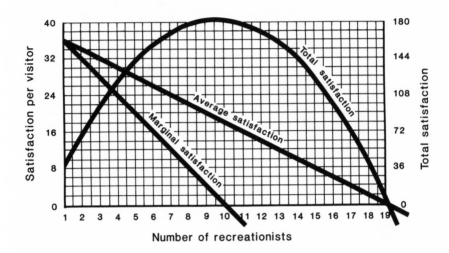

Figure 5-1.   Hypothetical relationship between increasing visitor use and satisfaction. (Adapted from Alldredge 1973)

Testing the Satisfaction Model

Empirical tests of the relationship between density and satisfaction have taken several forms. Probably the first test was conducted by Stankey (1973) as part of a larger survey of visitors to four wilderness areas. Visitors were asked to indicate how they felt about encountering an increasingly larger number of other parties, reporting their satisfaction on a five-point scale ranging from "very pleasant" to "very unpleasant." Satisfaction curves were then constructed showing the effect of increasing numbers of encounters with both backpackers and horseback riders on satisfaction (Figure 5-2). The curves generally support the satisfaction model as satisfaction falls nearly consistently, though not proportionally, through the range of other parties encountered. The data, however, were derived from hypothetical questions and further empirical testing was warranted.

Two tests of the satisfaction model conducted in the mid-1970s took an economic approach to the issue, closely following Alldredge's (1973) model. A sample of visitors to the Spanish Peaks Primitive Area, Montana, were given descriptions of five hypothetical wilderness trips in the study area (Cicchetti

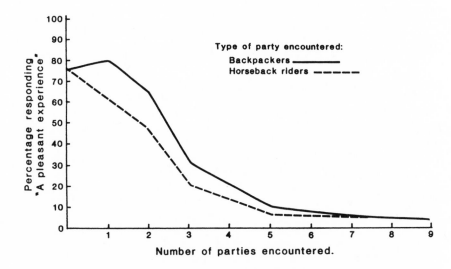

Figure 5-2. Satisfaction curves for encounters with hikers and horseback riders in three western wilderness areas. (From Stankey 1973)

and Smith 1973; Cicchetti 1976). Trips varied in the number of trail encounters per day and camp encounters per night, and length of stay, and respondents were asked to report the highest price they were willing to pay for each of the hypothetical trips. The survey was conducted by mail and received a low response rate—less than 50 percent. Moreover, approximately one-third of the visitors who did respond did not answer the questions concerning willingness to pay, many indicating they were unable to quantify their willingness to pay for wilderness recreation. Analysis of the findings showed no statistically significant relationship between willingness to pay and either trail encounters or camp encounters. Statistically controlling four other independent variables, the two encounter measures could be shown to reduce willingness to pay only slightly.

The second test using willingness to pay as a measure of satisfaction focused on visitors to six Rhode Island ocean beaches (McConnell 1977). Respondents were asked, among other things, how much they would have been willing to pay to come to the beach. Measurements were also taken of site conditions, including number of people per acre on the beach and air temperature. As in the previous study, initial analysis of the findings showed no statistically significant relationship between density (people per acre) and willingness to pay. Statistically controlling for three other independent variables, the partial correlation between density and willingness to pay was increased to a statistically significant level of .21 (α < .01), but this relationship varied substantially among the six beaches studied.

These studies tend to generate as much doubt as confidence in the relationship between density and satisfaction. The simple bivariate relationship between these variables assumed in the satisfaction model was not found in either study. Only after statistically controlling several other independent variables, a practice which would not be feasible under field conditions, could any significant relationship be demonstrated. Even under these conditions, the relationship varied by site. Both studies suffer from the shortcomings of the willingness to pay approach: it is often difficult to quantify the value of nonmarket goods such as wilderness recreation, and there are built-in biases to such questions if respondents think their answers will be used to formulate pricing policy. Finally, both studies were conducted under predominately hypothetical conditions.

More recently the satisfaction model has been tested under field conditions. Satisfaction has been measured under density conditions which vary naturally in recreation areas. The results of several studies conducted in this manner are summarized, to the extent they are comparable, in Table 5-2.

The most striking aspect of the table is the generally low relationships between variables. In many cases the relationships are not statistically significant. The strength of the relationships between density and satisfaction, for example, can best be described as low to moderate for two to four of the wilderness areas studied by Lucas (1980). In all other studies and areas where these variables were tested, relationships were weak or nonexistent. A moderately strong relationship between density and crowding was found in about half the areas where these variables were tested; other areas found a very weak relationship or none. The relationship between crowding and satisfaction was found to be generally weak or nonexistent. Lee (1977) found no relationship between perceived crowding and satisfaction as measured by intensity of greeting behavior along trails and extent of search behavior for appropriate campsites. Though the relationship for Colorado River rafters reported by Shelby (1980a) is statistically significant, it is very weak; perceived crowding explains only 2 percent of the variation in reported satisfaction.

Taken together, these studies, covering a variety of areas which range from rural rivers to national parks to wilderness, cast considerable doubt on the satisfaction model. Why are density and satisfaction seemingly so unrelated? The answer appears to lie in understanding of several conceptual and methodological issues.

Table 5-2.   Findings from empirical tests of the density-satisfaction relationship.

Study	Area	Users	Relationship between density and satisfaction	Relationship between density and crowding	Relationship between crowding and satisfaction
Heberlein 1977	Brule River, WI	Canoeists, tubers, fishermen	R = .009[a]		
Manning and Ciali 1980	4 Vermont rivers	Fishermen, floaters, swimmers	R = .14		
Lucas 1980	Desolation Wilderness, CA	Hikers	$\gamma = .17$[b]		
	Selway-Bitter-root Wilderness, ID and MT	Hikers, Horseback riders	$\gamma = .21$		
	Bob Marshall Wilderness Area, MT	Hikers, horseback riders	$\gamma = .26$		
	Cabinet Mtns. Wilderness, MT	Hikers, horseback riders	$\gamma = -.14$		
	Scapegoat Wilderness, MT	Hikers, horseback riders	$\gamma = .31$		
	Mission Mtns. Wilderness, MT	Hikers, horseback riders	$\gamma = .20$		
	Spanish Peaks Primitive Area, MT	Hikers, horseback riders	$\gamma = .11$		
	Great Bear Wilderness, MT	Hikers, horseback riders	$\gamma = -.08$		
	Jewel Basin Hiking Area, MT	Hikers, horseback riders	$\gamma = .08$		
Womble and Studebaker 1981	Katmai National Monument, AK	Developed area campers	$R^2 = .09$[c]	$R^2 = .07$	

Continued on page 56

Table 5-2. Findings from empirical tests of the density-satisfaction relationship.
(Cont.)

Study	Area	Users	Relationship between density and satisfaction	Relationship between density and crowding	Relationship between crowding and satisfaction
Hammitt et al. 1984	Hiawassee River, TN	Tubers		R = .61	
Absher and Lee 1981	Yosemite National Park, CA	Backpackers		R^2 = .07	
West 1982b	Ottawa National Forest, MI	Hikers		R^2 = .05	
Bultena et al. 1981b	Mt. McKinley National Park, AK	Hikers	R = −.01 −(−.06)	R = .33–.35	R = −.05
Titre and Mills 1982	Guadalupe River, TX	Floaters	No relationship using analysis of variance	Significant relationship using analysis of variance, but only on high use portion of the river.	
Lee 1975; 1977	Yosemite National Park, CA	Hikers, campers			No relationship between perceived crowding and behavioral measures of satisfaction.
Shelby 1980	Colorado River, Grand Canyon National Park, AZ	Rafters	R = .00[d] R = .05 R = .03 R = .01 R = −.01 R = .02	R = .05[d] R = .05 R = .05 R = .03 R = .12 R = .13	R = −.14
Shelby et al. 1983	Brule River, WI	Canoers		R^2 = .21	
	Wisconsin	Deer hunters		R^2 = .22	

Table 5-2.   Findings from empirical tests of the density-satisfaction relationship. (Cont.)

Study	Area	Users	Relationship between density and satisfaction	Relationship between density and crowding	Relationship between crowding and satisfaction
Shelby et al. 1983 (cont.)	Grand River Marsh, WI	Goose hunters (managed)		$R^2 = .03$	
	Grand River Marsh, WI	Goose hunters (firing line)		$R^2 = .23$	
	Rogue River, OR	Floaters		$R^2 = .02-.06$	
	Colorado River, Grand Canyon National Park, AZ	Floaters		$R^2 = .02$	
Vaske et al. 1982	Dolly Sods Wilderness Area, WV	Hikers		$R = .36$	

[a] R = product moment correlation efficient

[b] γ = gamma

[c] R^2 = multiple correlation coefficient

[d] The correlation coefficients in these columns are for the following six density/interaction variables: people per week leaving the put-in point; river contacts per day; people per day seen on the river; time in sight of people on the river; percent of all attraction sites with contact; and average number of people seen at attraction sites.

Expanding the Satisfaction Model

The density-satisfaction issue in outdoor recreation is a natural extension of a more general and long standing interest in crowding and human behavior. Marked increases in population growth over the last several decades have generated concern for potentially detrimental implications of high population density. Exploration of social dysfunctions related to population density has been the focus of a considerable body of social-psychological literature over the last fifty years. Application of the concepts developed in this literature to outdoor recreation (e.g., Heberlein 1977; Manning and Ciali 1980; Burch 1981; Gramann 1982) has proved instructive.

Both sociological and psychological studies of crowding have resulted in mixed findings. Early correlation studies often found statistically significant, positive relationships between population density and various indicators of social pathology such as criminal activity (Lottier 1938), mental illness (Faris and Dunham 1965), and marital dissatisfaction (Mitchell 1971). Experimental studies have been less consistent in their findings. Subjects exposed to high-density conditions have, in some studies (e.g., Griffitt and Veitch 1971; Valins and Baum 1973), exhibited more negative reactions than subjects exposed to low-density conditions. Other similar studies (e.g., Smith and Haythorn 1972; Freedman et al. 1971) have found no such effects.

Several theorists have speculated on the reasons for these mixed findings in crowding research. One line of reasoning suggests that a variety of coping mechanisms are evolved by individuals and groups (Altman 1975). When the environment becomes too densely populated, new behaviors are adopted which help relieve associated stress and anxiety. The classic work of Milgram (1970), for instance, has illustrated the ways in which urban residents cope with excessive, unwanted contacts—brusque conversations, unlisted telephones, and disregard of strangers, even when they may be in need.

Another line of reasoning distinguishes between the concepts of density and crowding (Stokols 1972a; 1972b). Density is a physical concept relating the idea of number of people per unit of space; it is strictly neutral and subject to no psychological or experiential evaluation or interpretation. Crowding, on the other hand, has a psychological meaning; it is a negative and subjective evaluation of a density level. Thus, density may increase to a point where it is perceived to interfere with one's activities or intentions, and at this point crowding occurs. Several social-psychological studies (e.g., Cohen et al. 1975; Desor 1972) indicate that crowding judgments are influenced by both the activities being pursued and the setting in which they occur. Thus, crowding appears to be a normative concept, dependent upon a variety of circumstances.

The coping and normative approaches to crowding suggested by the social-psychological literature have generated a number of hypotheses in outdoor recreation which help illuminate the relationship between density and satisfaction. These hypotheses and their empirical testing, along with some methodological issues introduced at the end of this section, have expanded the simple bivariate satisfaction model, whereby increased density causes decreased satisfaction, to a more comprehensive model as shown in Figure 5-3. The components of the model are described in the following paragraphs.

Coping Behavior. It is widely hypothesized that outdoor recreationists utilize two forms of coping behavior: displacement and rationalization.

Displacement. Many writers have suggested that as use densities increase some recreationists become dissatisfied and alter their patterns of recreation activity to avoid crowding, ultimately moving on to less densely used areas. In this manner, they are displaced by users more tolerant of higher densities. This

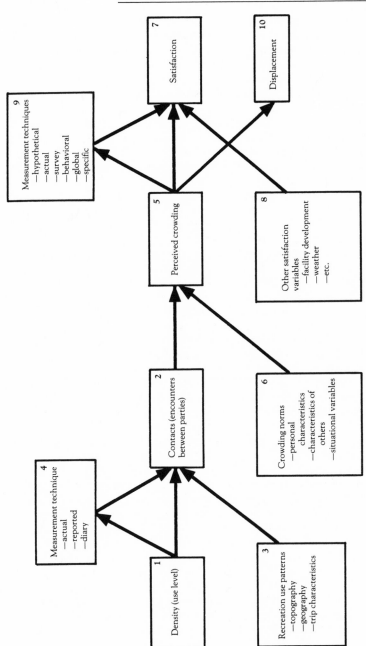

Figure 5-3. A crowding model.

suggests that the reason for a lack of relationship between density and perceived crowding is that people who are sensitive to existing density levels at each recreation site have been displaced from these sites. The displacement hypothesis was suggested as early as 1971 by Clark et al. who described it as a process of "invasion and succession."

A number of studies have addressed this hypothesis empirically. Several have focused on changes in behavior as related to density concerns. Rafters on the Colorado River in Grand Canyon National Park, for instance, changed their trip plans as a function of the density of river use (Neilson and Shelby 1977). Changes included limiting the number of attraction sites visited and the time spent at each, both actions designed to limit contact with other rafting parties.

Similarly, hikers in two wilderness areas reported changing the length and/or route of their trip because of use density: 25 percent in the Spanish Peaks Primitive Area, Montana, and 44 percent in the heavier used Desolation Wilderness Area, California (Stankey 1980a).

A slightly different methodology was applied in a study of visitors to the Boundary Waters Canoe Area, and indications of displacement were again found (Anderson 1980, 1983; Anderson and Brown 1984). Visitors who had made more than four trips to the area were studied to determine changes in trip patterns over time. The vast majority of respondents were found to have changed their pattern of use by selecting different entry points or campsites, or entering on a different day of the week. Factors related to trip changes included use density, litter, noise, and environmental impacts. In a similar study of boaters using the Apostle Islands National Lake Shore, Wisconsin, Vaske et al. (1980) found that boaters whose first trip to the area had occurred earlier evaluated existing contact levels more negatively than those whose first trip had occurred more recently, and also more frequently avoided the heavier used islands.

The final group of studies in this area has examined shifts in recreation sites. One (Becker 1981; Becker et al. 1981) studied recreation use of two rivers in the same geographic region. A subsample of users was identified who had purposively shifted use from one river to the other, at least partially in response to density conditions. In a different approach, Neilson and Endo (1977) studied a sample of private (non-commercial) river runners on the Colorado River, Grand Canyon National Park, 1959-1975. River-running histories were solicited from respondents. It was found that approximately 30 percent of the sample had shifted their river-running activities to rivers with a lower use level and might therefore be considered examples of the displacement process—though this is obviously speculative. Moreover, while the rivers to which these persons shifted were indeed less densely used, they were also closer to home, required less skill, involved shorter trips, and were less wild—which may simply be a function of the fact that there are few remote, wild rivers with low use levels available.

Two other studies have been suggestive of the displacement process. Wohlwill and Heft (1977) studied visitors to two recreation areas in Pennsylvania. One area, the Poconos, was substantially more developed than the other, Pine Creek. Users of the Pine Creek area were found to have traveled significantly longer distances, suggesting they had been forced to search out lower density areas. Users of the Poconos were much more supportive of high convenience facilities and high development levels. The authors suggest that a "positive feedback system" is in operation whereby initial use creates pressure for facilities which in turn attract more use, and so on. In this system users who prefer low development and use levels are easily displaced. This suggestion has been supported by a study of winter visitors to Great Smokey Mountains National Park (Hammitt and Hughes 1984); 78 percent of respondents reported they avoid backpacking in the park in the summer due to heavy use, and instead visit other lesser-used areas.

West's (1981a) study investigating displacement found no support for this hypothesis, however. An on-site survey of visitors to a Michigan site, coupled with a telephone survey of past visitors, found that past visitors who no longer used the area did not have greater perceptions of crowding that other categories of visitors. Nor was there any relationship between feeling crowded and intent to visit the area again.

Rationalization. Heberlein and Shelby (1977) hypothesize another coping behavior in outdoor recreation: a process of rationalization. Some people may rationalize and report that they had a good time regardless of conditions, since recreation activities are voluntarily selected and sometimes involve a substantial investment of time, money, and effort. This hypothesis is rooted in the theory of cognitive dissonance, developed by Festinger (1957) and others, and suggests that people tend to order their thoughts in ways that reduce inconsistencies and associated stress. Therefore, people may be inclined to rate their recreation experience high regardless of actual conditions to reduce internal conflict. This, then, may explain why reported satisfaction of recreationists is often not related to density levels.

This hypothesis appears reasonable when applied, as it originally was, to Colorado River/Grand Canyon users. For most people, this trip is a substantial undertaking: trips are long, normally requiring at least a week; commercial passengers pay high fees; and private trips may have to wait a year or considerably longer to receive a permit. Under these conditions, many people might refuse to be easily disappointed. The hypothesis loses some of its appeal, however, when applied to less extraordinary circumstances. Little support for this hypothesis, for example, was found in a study of river use in Vermont (Manning and Ciali 1980). Most visitors were in-state day users. With such a relatively small investment in their trip, it seems likely they would have admitted they had had an unsatisfactory experience because of crowding or for any other reason. Indeed, many respondents were not hesitant to express dissatisfaction, with reported satisfaction ratings ranging throughout the response scale.

Summary. Knowledge of coping behaviors of recreationists is not well developed. Evidence concerning the displacement hypothesis is not definitive. The ideal research approach—a longitudinal or panel study—has not yet been applied to this issue. However, the bulk of existing evidence is suggestive of changing trip patterns and, to some extent, shifts in areas used due to increasing use levels and associated effects. Therefore, a displacement component (box 10) has been added to the crowding model shown in Figure 5-3.

Because there is little evidence to support the hypothesis of rationalization and this hypothesized coping behavior may apply only under extraordinary circumstances, it is not included in the crowding model in Figure 5-3.

Normative Definitions of Crowding. The normative approach to crowding suggests that density is not interpreted negatively as crowding until it is perceived to interfere with or disrupt one's objectives or values. This approach has proved fertile for theory building and testing. A variety of factors have been suggested as forming the basis for crowding norms, among them personal characteristics of visitors, characteristics of others encountered, and situational variables.

Personal Characteristics of Visitors. Personal characteristics of visitors found to influence crowding norms include motivations for outdoor recreation, preferences and expectations for contacts, experience level, and attitudes toward management.

• *Motivations, preferences, and expectations.* Three of the personal characteristics of visitors which seem to be closely interrelated in this context are motivations for recreation[2] and preferences and expectations for contact. These factors have been included in several studies, the same study sometimes including two or even all three factors. The most comprehensive study (Ditton et al. 1983) surveyed recreationists on the Buffalo National River, Arkansas. Wide diversity in perceived crowding was found among the sample of river floaters and motivations for the trip were found to be significantly related to perceptions of crowding. Not surprisingly, respondents who felt crowded reported significantly higher ratings on the motivation "to get away from other people," while those whose enjoyment was enhanced by contacts reported significantly higher ratings on the motivations "to be a part of a group," "to have thrills and excitement," and "to share what I have learned with others." In addition, floaters who felt crowded reported lower fulfillment ratings for seven of the nine motivations tested. The survey also included questions on expected and preferred number of contacts. Mean scores comparing reported with expected contacts were consistently found to be significantly higher for respondents who

---

[2] Motivations for recreation are discussed in detail in Chapter Six.

felt crowded than for groups reporting neutral effect or increased enjoyment. Those who felt crowded were more likely to report having seen more people than expected. The same results were obtained for preferred contacts: those who felt crowded were distinguished from others by the fact that they tended to report experiencing more contacts than they preferred.

These results have been corroborated by all of the other studies addressing these factors. Absher and Lee (1981) included motivations in their study of the density-satisfaction relationship among backcountry hikers in Yosemite National Park. While density alone explained only 7 percent of the variation in perceived crowding (see Table 5-1), the addition of respondent ratings of seven trip motivations to the model increased the variance explained in perceived crowding to 23 percent. In particular, hikers who gave a relatively high rating to the motivation of "quietude" were more likely to perceive crowding, while those rating "nature involvement" and "shared experiences" high were less likely to perceive crowding. The other study relating motivations to perceptions of crowding (Roggenbuck and Schreyer 1977; Schreyer and Roggenbuck 1978) found that floaters on the Green and Yampa Rivers in Dinosaur National Monument who rated the motivations of "stress release/solitude" and "self-awareness" highly were more sensitive to higher use densities.

Other studies of this issue reported in Table 5-1 included a focus on expected and preferred contacts. Shelby's (1980a) study of Colorado River floaters found virtually no relationship between various density/interaction measures and perceived crowding (R ranged from .05 to .13). However, much higher correlations were found between perceived crowding and both expectations for contacts (R = −.30 and −.39, depending on the measure used) and preferences for contacts (R = −.40). Similarly, only a weak relationship was found between density and perceived crowding among campers at Katmai National Monument; density explained only 9 percent of the variation in perceived crowding (Womble and Studebaker 1981). However, expectations and preferences for density explained 20 and 37 percent, respectively, of the variation in perceived crowding. Bultena et al. (1981b) found moderately strong relationships between contacts experienced and feelings of crowding (R = .33 to .35, depending upon how contacts were measured) for hikers at Mount McKinley National Park, but stronger relationships were found between perceived crowding and preference for contacts (R = .45) and expectations for contacts (R = .42). A wide-ranging study of six areas supporting a variety of recreation activities found that by adding expectations and preferences for contacts to actual contacts, the amount of variance in perceived crowding explained was increased by 5 to 19 percent across the areas studied (Shelby et al. 1983). Expectations tended to show a more consistent effect on crowding than did preferences. Similar findings were reported by a study of visitors to an eastern wilderness area (Vaske et al. 1982).

A related issue found in the literature is the suggestion that some visitors who are new to an activity or area have little or no expectation about the conditions they will find, including density levels (Nielson and Shelby 1977; Nielson et al. 1977). Schreyer et al. (1976) refer to this issue as the "floating baseline" effect; first-time users tend to accept what they find as normal, whereas repeat visitors evaluate what they find against past experience. West (1981a) terms this notion the "uninitiated newcomer" hypothesis. This hypothesis might help explain the lack of relationship between density and satisfaction, as crowding norms and expectations are likely to be shaped by the use densities found. However, like the coping behavior of rationalization discussed in the previous section, this hypothesis appears most reasonable when applied to "once in a lifetime" areas and activities, but seems less broadly applicable to less extraordinary areas and activities where newcomers generally comprise only a small percentage of all visitors. Moreover, the studies described above indicate that most recreationists, regardless of experience, are able to report expectations for contact levels. West's (1981a) study of this issue found no differences in crowding perceptions between newcomers and longer-time users.

A second related issue is that areas and activities are self-selected by recreationists to meet preferences and expectations, including those concerning use density. Consequently, it might be expected that visitors would generally be satisfied regardless of use density. The generally high levels of satisfaction found in many outdoor recreation studies are supportive of this hypothesis. More directly supportive are two studies which indicate visitors tend to select recreation sites which are in line with their preferences and expectations about density and related conditions (Becker 1978; Greenleaf et al. 1984). Both studies found that hikers in the lowest use zone tended to be the least tolerant of contact with others.

This hypothesis begins to break down, however, as opportunities for outdoor recreation, particularly low-density alternatives, become limited. Recreationists may use a particular area even though use density is higher than preferred or expected because there are no reasonable alternatives available. Several of the studies described above found a substantial number, though still a minority, of visitors to be dissatisfied with use density and this may be indicative of limited alternatives for low-density recreation. This situation may well become more prevalent as participation in outdoor recreation continues to rise.

• *Experience.* While the studies described above have focused considerable attention on motives, preferences, and expectations, perhaps the most widely studied personal characteristic thought to influence crowding norms is experience. Experience level is thought to affect normative definitions of crowding either through refinement of tastes (Krutilla 1967; Munley and Smith 1976; Bryan 1977) or by virtue of exposure to lower density conditions as a result of earlier participation. The bulk of the empirical evidence supports the notion that more experienced users are more sensitive to higher use densities. This appears true regardless of how experience is measured: general experience in the activity, rate of participation, experience on-site, or some other dimension.[3] Two studies (Vaske et al. 1980; Ditton et al. 1983) previously described found a positive relationship between experience and sensitivity to crowding, the first with regard to experience on-site and the second across several measures of experience. Towler (1977) also found that backcountry hikers in Grand Canyon National Park with more on-site experience had a greater desire to be alone along with other more "purist" views. Murray (1974) found that more experienced Appalachian Trail hikers expressed stronger preferences for low-density hiking. And Heberlein and Dunwiddie (1979), in a study of visitors to the Bridger Wilderness Area, Wyoming, observed that more experienced campers tended to select campsites farther from other campers.

Two other studies found a relationship between density/crowding and experience which conflicts with previous studies, but the relationships were generally not strong. Stankey (1980a) tested for the effect of general wilderness experience on the satisfaction curves described earlier in this chapter. No effects were found except that more experienced visitors to the Spanish Peaks Primitive Area indicated a greater tolerance for encountering large parties. And the study of backpackers in Yosemite National Park by Absher and Lee (1981) found a very weak and not statistically significant correlation (R = .03) between general backcountry camping experience and perceived crowding.

• *Attitudes.* Attitudes towards wilderness and the extent to which attitudes conform with values suggested in the Wilderness Act ("wilderness purism") have also been found to affect normative definitions of crowding. Both studies which have applied a wilderness purism scale to the issue of crowding have found that it distinguishes among respondents with respect to perceptions of crowding. The satisfaction curves derived by Stankey (1973) from wilderness users were found to be distinctly different for strong purists and average visitors. For strong purists, satisfaction dropped off both more quickly and more steeply. And under field conditions, Schreyer and Roggenbuck's (1978) study of floaters on the Green and Yampa Rivers found that those with the most purist attitudes consistently registered a higher degree of perceived crowding at each encounter level.

• *Demographics.* It has also been suggested that demographic characteristics affect crowding norms, but these relationships have only been reported in one study which found no statistically significant relationship between age, sex, or

---

[3] Several studies have developed sophisticated treatments of recreation experience, combining and testing a variety of measures. Hammitt and McDonald (1983) have developed an index combining several measures of recreation experience. Two studies of river recreationists (Schreyer and Lime 1984; Schreyer et al. 1984) have integrated a variety of experience measures and tested their effect on area and trip evaluations. Each of these studies has found that experience level has statistically significant effects on selected visitor attitudes and perceptions, though none of the studies has addressed perceived crowding directly.

education level of the respondents and perceived crowding (Absher and Lee 1981).

• *Summary.* The bulk of the empirical evidence suggests the notion that motivations for recreation, preferences and expectations for contacts with others, and experience level and attitudes do influence the point at which increasing use density is negatively interpreted as crowding. These factors have therefore been included (box 6) in the crowding model (Figure 5-3).

Characteristics of Those Encountered. There is considerable evidence that the characteristics of those encountered also affect crowding norms. Factors found important include type and size of group, behavior, and the degree to which groups are perceived to be alike.

• *Type and size of group.* Studies of conflict between types of groups in the outdoors are legion (e.g. Devall and Harry 1981; Driver and Bassett 1975; Sheridan 1979; Baldwin 1970; Dunn 1970; Jackson and Wong 1982; Jacob and Schreyer 1980; Shelby 1980b; Knopp and Tyger 1973; McCay and Moeller 1976; Noe et al. 1981; Noe et al. 1982). It seems only reasonable to think that tolerance for meeting another group would depend, at least to some extent, on its characteristics. Several studies support this view empirically, with the type of group most often defined in terms of mode of travel. Lucas's (1964b; 1964c) early study in the Boundary Waters Canoe Area found that paddling canoeists distinguished sharply among the three types of area users when asked their reactions to meeting other groups. They disliked encountering motorboats, were less resentful of encountering motorized canoes, and were relatively tolerant of encountering at least some other paddled canoes. Motor canoeists made similar distinctions, though not as sharply. Thus, canoeists felt crowded at much lower levels of use where motorboats were present.

Stankey (1973; 1980a) also found differential crowding effects based on mode of travel. The satisfaction curves shown in Figure 5-2 demonstrate different tolerances for encountering backpackers and horseback riders along wilderness trails. Similar differences in satisfaction curves were found for paddling canoeists, motor canoeists, and motorboaters in the Boundary Waters Canoe Area, corroborating the findings of Lucas. Compatibility indexes have also been developed for four types of trail users—hikers, horseback riders, bicycle riders, and motorcycle riders—by asking respondents how desirable it would be to encounter other types of trail users (McCay and Moeller 1976). The highest compatibility ratings for three of the four types were for meeting their own kind.

Lime (1972b) has suggested that party size also affects crowding norms. Considerable support has been found for this notion; a majority of wilderness users said they would prefer to see five small parties during the day rather than one large party (Stankey 1973).

• *Behavior.* The behavior of other groups also seems to affect crowding norms. Driver and Bassett (1975) found that about half of fishermen and streamside residents sampled on the Au Sable River, Michigan, objected to seeing canoeists; however, they objected primarily because of inconsiderate behavior, such as yelling or shouting, rather than sheer numbers. There was substantial objection to the behavior of groups exceeding ten canoes. West (1982b) conducted a more detailed study of behavior and its relationship to perceived crowding. His study of national forest hikers found that 30.9 percent were bothered by other users. Probing more deeply, it was found that of this total, 56.9 percent were bothered by the behavior of others, 31.4 percent by the number of others encountered, and 4.1 percent by different types of users. Specific forms of behavior reported as bothering respondents were, in decreasing order: noise, yelling, and loud behavior; littering and polluting lakes; and noncompliance with rules. Respondents exposed to high perceived density (those reporting ten or more contacts) and negative behavior felt crowded 47.9 percent of the time, while respondents exposed to high perceived density but not negative behavior felt crowded only 16.7 percent of the time. Finally, Titre and Mills (1982) asked floaters on the Guadalupe River, Texas, to report both the number of encounters with other groups and whether these encounters were considered disruptive, enhancing, or neutral. The number of disruptive encounters was found to be a more consistent predictor of perceived crowding than any other measure, including simple perceived density. No effort was made, however, to define why an encounter was perceived as disruptive.

• *Perceptions of alikeness.* The third characteristic of other groups that seems to affect crowding norms is the degree to which groups are perceived as being alike. This factor appears closely related to behavior, but is more difficult to measure and study. Consequently it has been addressed more often on a theoretical basis than in the field.

In Chapter Two it was noted that the vast majority of people participate in outdoor recreation in family and/or friendship groups. This suggests the notion of solitude so often associated with certain types of outdoor recreation may not mean simple isolation from others. It also suggests an inward focus on interpersonal relationships within the social group. Both of these notions are ultimately important in the concept of alikeness.

Twight et al. (1981) and Hammitt (1982) have developed conceptual analyses of solitude and privacy as applied to outdoor recreation. Borrowing on the theoretical work of social-psychologists (Westin 1967; Pastalan 1970; Marshall 1972, 1974), several dimensions of solitude and/or privacy were revealed:

1. Intimacy: an attempt to achieve interpersonal relationships between or among members of a small group of selected members.
2. Solitude: a desire to be alone at times without interruptions.
3. Anonymity: a desire for freedom from identification in a public setting.

4. Reserve: a preference to avoid self-disclosure, particularly to those other than close friends.

5. Seclusion: the visual and auditory seclusion of one's home (campsite, etc.) from neighbors and traffic.

6. Not neighboring: a feeling that visitation by neighbors and choice of friends should be controlled.

Scales were developed to empirically test the application of these dimensions of solitude to outdoor recreation.

Twight et al. (1981) surveyed users of a developed campground in Shenandoah National Park and backpackers in the Allegheny National Forest, Pennsylvania, asking them to rate the importance of various solitude dimensions. Backpackers were found to score higher to a statistically significant degree than developed area campers in the dimensions of intimacy, solitude, anonymity, and seclusion, though the differences in general were not great. The differences in scores on intimacy were the largest, with backpackers rating this dimension of solitude significantly higher than developed area campers. This indicates the potential importance of intimacy with groups in more primitive types of outdoor recreation. Hammitt (1982) surveyed college student backpackers to test the importance of a number of dimensions of solitude to wilderness recreation. Items found of greatest importance involved freedom of choice in one's own actions, thoughts, and use of time, and a natural environment free from human influence. Items receiving the lowest ratings had to do with the isolated, individualistic nature of solitude.

Thus, solitude in outdoor recreation may have more to do with interaction among group members free from disruptions than with actual isolation. This suggests that as long as contacts with other groups are not considered disturbing they do not engender feelings of crowding or dissatisfaction. And this in turn suggests the notion of alikeness.

Lee has done much to further the notion of alikeness among recreation groups. In an early study of the social definition of outdoor recreation places (Lee 1972), a variety of park environments were observed to be highly ordered social systems which help to ensure predictable forms of behavior. Contrary to their conventional image as free and unregulated spaces, park environments are governed by practical and informal behavioral norms based on regularities in meaning and use assigned by user groups. Deviations from these norms are often viewed with suspicion and anxiety. Lee concludes from this study that "individuals seek outdoor areas where they may share a scheme of order with others similar enough to themselves to be able to take for granted many everyday normative constraints." In this context, the number of users present is not so important as a shared system of values and behavioral norms.

In a follow-up study of backpackers in Yosemite National Park, Lee (1975, 1977) elaborates on this line of reasoning. As reported in Table 5-1, no relationship was found in this study between perceived crowding and behavioral measures of satisfaction. Lee attributes this finding to the idea that most social interaction between groups in outdoor recreation settings is conducted with little conscious deliberation or, in more technical terms, in nonsymbolic modes of communication. Blumer (1936) defines such communication as "spontaneous and direct responses to the gestures of the other individual, without the intermediation of any interpretation." People are therefore largely unaware of such social interaction, and it has little effect on perceptions of crowding. Lee concludes that the quality of a recreational experience "appears to be closely linked with the opportunity to take for granted the behavior of other visitors," and that "an essential ingredient for such an experience [is] the assumption that other visitors are very much like oneself, and will, therefore, behave in a similar manner." Thus, to the extent that groups are perceived as alike and require little conscious attention, encounters have limited disruptive effects on intimacy and other dimensions of solitude desired by social groups.

The importance of perceptions of alikeness is emphasized by Cheek and Burch (1976) who point out the lack of well-established behavioral norms within wildland types of outdoor recreation. Few of the physical and institutional screens of everyday life—walls, gates, neighborhoods—are present to segregate groups who wish to limit contact. Social norms are also lacking:

> Unlike golf and other organized sports, which have normative mechanisms for including strangers in the play, wilderness camping is especially fluid. Wilderness camping has no clear and validated rules regarding roles, goals, and relationships, except those already established within the intimate group. Consequently, strangers are disruptive because there is no context within which they can be fit (Cheek and Burch 1976, p. 168).

The inward focus of the social group and concerns for alikeness between groups is illustrated in an observational study of fishing and other recreation behavior at high-mountain lakes in Washington State (Hendee et al. 1977). It was observed that 80 percent of fishermen carried out most of their fishing activity within about 20 feet of a companion, but 75 percent remained 100 feet or more from people in other parties. Similarly, all but 10 percent of fishermen engaged in at least some conversation with companions while fishing, but more than 90 percent did not converse with anyone from another party. Moreover, the limited conversation that did occur between parties was "often probing as if to determine the extent to which parties shared motives, interests, or expertise that might serve as the basis for continuing the contact" (Hendee et al. 1977).

One other empirically-based study has examined the notion of alikeness among recreation parties. Earlier in this chapter Lucas's (1964b) study of visitors to the Boundary Waters Canoe Area in the early 1960s was described, and it was noted that paddling canoeists generally disliked encountering motorboaters, but that the reverse was generally not true. Adelman et al. (1982) termed this phenomenon "asymetric antipathy" and reexamined the study area to see if this conflict pattern persisted over time. Closely replicating the research methods of Lucas, very similar results were obtained: 71 percent of paddlers disliked meeting and/or seeing motorboat users, while only 8 percent of the motorboat users disliked meeting and/or seeing paddlers. The study went on to assess the perceived similarity of each group of users to the other. The majority of motorboaters perceived paddling canoeists as similar to themselves, while the majority of paddling canoeists perceived motorboaters as dissimilar to themselves. This relationship held over all measures of perceived similarity. Thus, it appears that perceptions of similarity or alikeness between recreation groups may be closely associated with normative definitions of crowding.

Initial judgments on alikeness between groups are almost certainly made on the basis of outward appearances such as group structure (e.g., size), activities (e.g., mode of travel), behavior (e.g., littering and noise), and possibly even physical manifestations (e.g., type of equipment). Knopp and Tyger (1973) found that, "Recreation activities often serve as a symbolic identification for a cultural group." And Burch suggests that values are often expressed and interpreted in society at large in such shorthand notations:

> Such patterns are not unlike the visual symbols of counterculturists, soul brothers, decal-flagged middle-Americans who announce a shared value system which brings them together by setting them apart from other social groups (Burch 1974, p. 96).

• *Summary.* Several characteristics of those encountered in outdoor recreation areas affect normative definitions of crowding. When others are encountered who are viewed as inappropriate or different in unfavorable ways, crowding is perceived at relatively low levels of contact. Pertinent characteristics of those encountered include type and size of group, behavior, and perceptions of alikeness. These factors have been added (box 6) to the crowding model in Figure 5-3.

Situational Variables. The environment in which encounters occur apparently influences, to some extent, the ways in which those encounters are perceived and evaluated. Important variables include the type of recreation area, location within an area, and environmental design and quality.

• *Type of area.* Clawson and Knetsch (1966) suggested very early that there are inter-area differences in crowding norms. Hypothetical curves relating the effects of density to recreation quality were seen as taking dramatically different shapes for three types of recreation areas: wilderness, an unimproved campground, and a highly developed campground. That different use levels are appropriate for different types of recreation areas seems obvious in a conceptual way, though not much is known about the issue in a quantitative sense. Empirical evidence is offered by McConnell's (1977) study of density and crowding (measured as willingness to pay) which found different relationships at different types of beaches ranging from a natural area to a highly developed "singles" beach. Manning and Ciali (1981) also found different patterns of desired use density among users of six river types ranging from primitive torrent to urban meander.

• *Location within an area.* More focus has been placed on intra-area differences in crowding norms. The most consistent finding has been high sensitivity to encounters associated with campsite location. Burch and Wenger (1967), for example, found that two-thirds of wilderness visitors preferred a campsite far away from others. Stankey (1973; 1980) also found wilderness visitors sensitive to campsite encounters. The vast majority of respondents (75 percent) agreed with the statement, "When staying out overnight in the wilderness, it is most enjoyable not to be near anyone else." Visitors also reported higher sensitivity to encounters at campsites than along trails. Lucas (1980a) reports similar findings: the large majority of visitors to nine wilderness areas preferred to camp alone. The only empirical evidence which varies from this pattern is Ditton et al.'s. (1983) study of river users which found that campground encounters had little effect on perceived crowding; however, these were campgrounds occupied before and after a float trip, which may explain their lack of significance. A higher sensitivity to use levels at campsites reflects the importance of the campsite in recreation activity patterns. Campers in both developed and backcountry areas spend the majority of their waking hours in and around the campsite (King 1966; Hendee et al. 1977).

Heightened sensitivity to encounters has also been found in the interior of wilderness as opposed to the periphery (Stankey 1973). Given the choice, 68 percent of wilderness visitors expressed a preference for encounters to occur within the first few miles from the road rather than interior zones.

• *Environmental factors.* Hammitt (1983) has suggested that crowding may also depend on the physical, non-human environment. An office, for example, can be perceived as crowded because the amount and configuration of furnishings prohibit one from functioning as desired, even when no one else is present. This notion has been termed "environmental affordances" (Gibson 1977; 1979), and "functional density" (Rapoport 1975) in the general social-psychological literature. This issue has received little research attention, though Womble and Studebaker's (1981) study of crowding in a national park campground is suggestive. This study, as reported in Table 5-2, found very little relationship between density and perceived crowding. However, the authors went on to explore the open-ended comments section of the questionnaire in an effort to identify other factors which might account for unexplained variance in crowding perceptions. Several factors were identified, the most important of which were proximity of campsites and insufficient facilities. This suggests design aspects of the recreation environment may be involved in normative definitions of crowding.

A related consideration is the perceived quality of the recreation environment. Vaske et al. (1982) created an index of perceived environmental disturbance for visitors to the Dolly Sods Wilderness Area, West Virginia. The index was comprised of six items for which respondents rated perceived conditions as worse than, about the same as, or better than expected. In keeping with other studies investigating visitor perceptions of environmental impacts, as reported in Chapter Three, the overall index indicated that visitors generally found environmental conditions about the same or slightly better than expected. However, some respondents rated conditions worse than expected, and this had a substantive effect on perceived crowding. When the perceived environmental disturbance index was added to measures of reported, preferred, and expected contacts, the amount of variance explained in perceived crowding rose from 23 percent to 33 percent. Moreover, the index had the largest effect on perceived crowding of any of the four independent variables. These findings indicate that perceived crowding is influenced not only by the physical presence of others, but also by the environmental impacts left by previous visitors. These findings are consistent with other studies which indicate that visitors are often more disturbed by the presence of litter or other environment degradation than by contacts with other parties (Stankey 1973; Lee 1975; Lucas 1980).

• *Summary.* Situational variables can affect normative definitions of crowding. That is, the environment in which encounters occur, as defined by the type of recreation area, the location within an area, design considerations, and perceived environmental quality help to determine when and where density is perceived as crowding. These factors have been added (box 6) to the crowding model in Figure 5-3.

Methodological Issues. Investigations of the relationships between density, crowding, and satisfaction have brought to light several important methodological issues which potentially affect these relationships. These include the distinction between use density and contacts, alternative measures of contacts, the multidimensional nature of satisfaction, consistency of satisfaction measures, and the need for behavioral measures of crowding and satisfaction.

Density and Contacts. The first issue concerns the relationship between density and contacts or encounters. It is often implicitly assumed that increased density results in proportional increases in contacts. But the limited research into this issue indicates otherwise. Density of floaters on the Colorado River in Grand Canyon (defined as the number of people per week leaving the principal put-in point) was measured simultaneously with contact levels between parties (Neilson and Shelby 1977; Neilson et al. 1977; Shelby 1980a). The variables were positively related to a high degree, but density explained only about half the variation in contact levels. Bultena et al. (1981b) report an even lower relationship between density and contacts in the backcountry of Mount McKinley National Park. The unexplained variance in contact levels may be due to the complexity and randomness of trip patterns, intervening structural elements of topography and geography which limit contacts, purposive behavior to avoid contacts as use levels increase, and other unknown factors. It should be remembered from Chapter Two that recreation use patterns tend to be highly uneven over both space and time. Moreover, it was reported earlier in this chapter that in several studies visitors have reported changing the length and route of their trips in response to density levels. Both of these findings may help explain the lower relationship between density and crowding than might have intuitively been expected. These findings suggest the need for a research and management emphasis on measuring contacts in addition to density. While density measures are more readily available, it is contacts with other parties that visitors experience and which are likely to affect perceived crowding and satisfaction.

Measuring Contacts. A related issue concerns how contacts are measured. Three techniques are found in the literature: actual contacts—recorded by a participant observer (Shelby 1980a); reported contacts—self-reports by respondents after the outing (e.g. Manning and Ciali 1980); and diary contacts—self-reports by respondents recorded during the outing (McCool et al. 1977). Shelby and Colvin (1982) have compared the three measures using samples of river floaters on the Rogue River and the Illinois River, both in Oregon. Users who experienced fewer than six contacts were generally accurate (by comparison with actual contacts) in reporting them, but at higher levels of contact most users reported only about half as many contacts as actually occurred. Reported and diary contacts were found to be in close agreement. Thus, in low density recreation areas, self-reported contacts can probably be relied upon as reasonably accurate and should generally be used due to the administrative difficulties and potential intrusion on the visitors' experience represented by diaries. But in relatively high density areas, reported and diary contacts must be used with caution. Unfortunately, actual contacts are usually difficult and expensive to measure. However, the potential usefulness of reported and diary contacts should not be overlooked, even when they are known to be inaccurate. Self-reports represent the visitors' perceived reality and this can be important in assessing recreation quality.

Multidimensional Nature of Satisfaction. Perhaps the most important methodological issue concerning the relationships discussed in this chapter is measurement of satisfaction. The bivariate satisfaction model discussed early in this chapter suggests that satisfaction is simply a function of density: in fact, as was noted in Chapter One, satisfaction is a complex, multidimensional concept. The earliest attempt at testing the satisfaction model hints at this issue. In none of the satisfaction curves developed by Stankey (1973) (such as that in Figure 5-2) does satisfaction reach its theoretical scaled maximum—even when the level of encounters is zero. Similar results were obtained by Manning and Ciali (1980). Clearly, factors other than density must contribute to satisfaction.

The studies reported in Table 5-2 suggest this more directly, particularly those of Lee (1975) and Shelby (1980a). In these studies, feelings of being crowded had little or no effect on satisfaction. Both studies go on to identify a number of diverse variables which are correlated with satisfaction, including

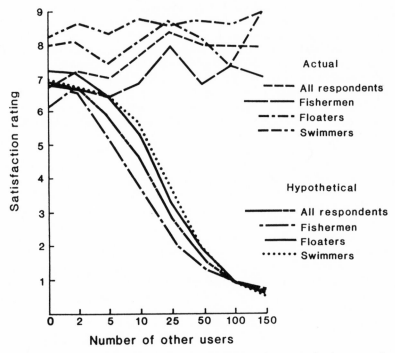

The scale of the X axis is not proportional, and is drawn this way to keep the data points from being too highly skewed toward the origin.

Figure 5-4.   Relationship between use density and satisfaction under hypothetical and actual conditions. (From Manning and Ciali 1980)

absence of litter and other pollution, low level of facility development, pleasant social demeanor of others, and good physical condition of the trail.

The problem of measuring satisfaction as a function of density or perceived crowding is illustrated by Manning and Ciali (1980) (Figure 5-4). In this study the relationship between density and satisfaction was measured under both actual field conditions and the hypothetical convention used by Stankey (1973; 1980a) whereby respondents are implicitly asked to assume away all other factors and to focus only on the two variables under consideration. Using the latter method, a clear negative relationship was found, but caution should be used in interpreting such findings and incorporating them into management policy. Research results from this idealized and rigorous world of fixed external variables may not hold under more complex field conditions. Tested under actual field conditions, no relationship was found between density and satisfaction; but once again, caution must be used in interpreting these results. The absence of relationships may be due to masking by more powerful but unknown variables, such as weather conditions.

The potentially complex effects of density on satisfaction have also been illustrated in a study of deer hunting (Heberlein et al. 1982). Density of hunters was found to have both positive and negative effects on overall satisfaction. Increased hunter density results in more deer seen per hunter (as more deer are moved through the area) and this has a positive effect on satisfaction. However, increased hunter density also results in more interference among hunters and this detracts from satisfaction.

Ditton et al. (1981) suggest that a multiple-item approach to measuring satisfaction may help resolve this dilemma, and developed and tested a five-item satisfaction scale in their study of floaters on the Buffalo National River, Arkansas. Results indicated that a better model of overall satisfaction could be obtained with the multiple-item scale than with any of the individual scale items. Moreover, different independent variables entered the regression models for each of the individual satisfaction scale items, indicating that each item was tapping a somewhat different dimension of satisfaction. Shelby et al. (1980) endorse the notion that single, global measures of satisfaction are generally inadequate. In most cases researchers and managers are interested in evaluating the effects on users of a single attribute such as contact level, and global measures of satisfaction are generally too far removed from single attributes to be effective evaluation measures. Empirical findings tend to support this notion. A detailed study of satisfaction among campers measured satisfaction for individual attributes of the camping experience in addition to overall satisfaction (Dorfman 1979). Though overall satisfaction was correlated with other measures of satisfaction to a statistically significant degree (R generally ranged between .30 and .60), it is clear these variables were not measuring the identical concept.

Consistency of Satisfaction Measures. Related to this issue are questions of timing, content, and context of satisfaction measures. A study of wilderness visitors by Peterson and Lime (1973) demonstrated that there were differences in satisfaction between respondents interviewed on-site and the same people surveyed later at home by mail: evaluations of the trip became more positive over time. The differences might be explained using the rationalization process described in the section on coping behaviors (see page 61). As time passes negative evaluations fade to minimize cognitive dissonance. Differences in reported satisfaction have also been found as a function of questionnaire content and context (Schomaker and Knopf 1982a; 1982b). Alternative wording of questions designed to measure satisfaction have been found to result in significantly different satisfaction scores. And when satisfaction measures were intermixed with questions evaluating specific aspects of the trip, average satisfaction scores were lower than when the satisfaction measures were presented alone. There is little to indicate what approach to either of these issues is "better." Rather, the key seems to be consistency; the approach used should be as consistent as possible, especially when results are to be compared between areas or over time (Knopf and Lime 1981; Lime et al. 1981).

The Need for Behavioral Measures. A final methodological issue concerns the need for behavioral measures of crowding and satisfaction or, more precisely, multiple measurement approaches. Research in outdoor recreation has been dominated by survey methods. A review of methodological approaches employed in studies published in the *Journal of Leisure Research*, for example, found that 94 percent used survey techniques (Riddick et al. 1984). While survey methods can be exceedingly useful, their potential shortcomings are well documented, particularly the potential weakness of the assumption that attitudes are closely related to behavior (e.g. Clark 1977; Wicker 1969; Deutscher 1966; Heberlein 1973). Two studies on the crowding issue point out this potential weakness. Lee (1977) found that even though many respondents reported feeling crowded, observations of their behavior indicated little or no effort to achieve additional privacy. This result obviously calls into question the validity of self-reports on crowding in this case (and perhaps others as well). West (1981b) also raises questions about self-reports or surveys of crowding perceptions. His survey of national forest backpackers found 22 percent reporting feelings of crowding, but 70 percent of this subsample was not in favor of lowering permitted use levels.

These findings suggest a more diversified research approach in outdoor recreation. While behavioral measures of outdoor recreation through techniques such as observation also have potential weaknesses (Webb et al. 1966; Campbell 1970), these are different from those of the survey approach. The best solution is therefore to apply both research approaches, using each to validate the other.

Summary. Several methodological issues affect the relationships between density, crowding, and satisfaction. These issues involve the ways in which these variables are conceptualized and measured. These factors have been added (boxes 3, 4, 8, and 9) to the crowding model in Figure 5-3.

An Expanded Crowding Model. The issues discussed in this section are incorporated in the crowding model in Figure 5-3. The discussion has been long and winding, but has resulted in a more comprehensive and realistic picture of crowding in outdoor recreation. The expanded model recognizes that density of recreation use (box 1) results in contacts between parties (box 2), but that other variables affect contacts as well, including topography, geography, and the complexities of trip patterns (box 3). Moreover, the way in which contacts are measured will affect the ultimate number derived (box 4). Second, the model shows that contacts between parties affect perceived crowding (box 5), but so does the way in which these contacts are interpreted (box 6). Crowding norms based on personal characteristics of visitors, the characteristics of those encountered, and situational variables affect the point at which contacts are evaluated negatively. Third, perceived crowding affects overall satisfaction (box 7), but is only one of theoretically many variables to do so (box 8). Moreover, the relationship between perceived crowding and satisfaction depends on measurement techniques (box 9). And feelings of perceived crowding can result in displacement of some users (box 10) so their satisfaction ratings are not measured.

Summary and Conclusions

1. *There has been long-standing concern over the effect of increasing use density on the quality of the recreation experience.*

2. *This concern over use density has been based on an assumed inverse relationship between density and satisfaction, sometimes called the "satisfaction model."*

3. *Empirical tests have generally found little, if any, statistical relationship between density, crowding, or satisfaction.*

4. *Reasons for this lack of relationship include coping behavior of recreationists, normative definitions of crowding, and several methodological issues. More specifically, these reasons are:*

   A. *Visitors sensitive to density may be displaced to other sites by visitors less sensitive to density.*

   B. *Personal characteristics of visitors influence when density is evaluated as crowding. These characteristics include motivations, preferences, expectations, experience, and attitudes.*

   C. *The characteristics of others encountered influence when density is evaluated as crowding. These characteristics include type and size of group, behavior, and perceptions of alikeness.*

   D. *The situation in which encounters occur influences when density is evaluated as crowding. These factors include type of recreation area, location within the area, design considerations, and perceived environmental quality.*

   E. *Contacts between recreation parties are not solely a function of use density.*

   F. *Contacts between recreation parties may vary depending upon whether they are measured objectively by observers or self-reported by visitors.*

   G. *Satisfaction is a multi-faceted concept, influenced only partially by perceptions of crowding.*

   H. *The relationship between crowding and satisfaction depends upon how satisfaction is measured: hypothetically or under field conditions; through survey or behavioral approaches; and globally or specifically.*

5. The way in which the above items influence the relationship between density and satisfaction is shown schematically in Figure 5-3.

6. Longitudinal study of the process of displacement is needed.

7. Satisfaction is not a proper criterion for managing density and crowding in recreation areas. If the process of displacement is operating or if in some other way the population of visitors is changing, satisfaction is likely to remain high despite changing density conditions. The ultimate result will be loss of diversity in outdoor recreation opportunities, particularly low-density alternatives.

8. More research is needed into what constitutes perceptions of alikeness between recreation parties. Inherent in this issue is why visitors often don't report all of the actual contacts they experience.

9. There is considerable diversity among the public about appropriate contact levels.

10. Recreation areas and zones should be managed to encourage relatively homogeneous groups in terms of party type and size, behavior, and other factors which contribute to perceptions of alikeness.

11. Management and research attention should be focused on contact levels in addition to more readily available density or overall use level. Contacts are more directly related to perceptions of crowding than density of use. Moreover, spatial and temporal use patterns might be managed to reduce contacts without affecting overall use levels.

12. Global measures of satisfaction are generally not appropriate for either research or management purposes. More attribute-specific satisfaction measures are needed.

13. Measurement of density, crowding, and satisfaction related variables should be as consistent as possible between areas and over time.

14. "Solitude" in outdoor recreation has several meanings in addition to the traditional concept of isolation. In particular, opportunities for intimacy within groups is important.

Chapter Six

Motivations for Recreation: A Behavioral Approach

Early Explorations

Early empirical research in outdoor recreation, like that in all emerging areas of study, was primarily descriptive, focusing on the activities and socio-economic and cultural characteristics of users, and their attitudes and preferences about management. But even as this descriptive base of information was being built there were early signs of an analytical interest in recreation, specifically the question of why people participate in outdoor recreation. This interest germinated in the 1960s, blossomed in the 1970s, and continues to flourish today, expanding into new areas.

Illustrative of the early interest in motivations for outdoor recreation was the work of Bultena and Taves (1961) in the Quetico-Superior Area, Minnesota. Observing that fishermen returning to camp with empty creels were not dissatisfied with their visit to the area, they hypothesized that there must be multiple motives involved in outdoor recreation. Tentative support for this hypothesis was found in an exploratory element of this study which asked visitors to the area to rate the importance of seventeen potential motivations for their visits. Results indicated that visitors to the area tended to think of their trips as a means of escaping familiar routines and the cares associated with living in an urbanized society, though none of the motivations was rated as very important by the majority of visitors. The Outdoor Recreation Resources Review Commission also included a study component exploring the motivations of visitors to three wilderness areas (Wildland Research Center 1962). Results were highly variable, though the two strongest motivations across the sample were a wish to escape from the routines and crowds of daily life, and a desire to enjoy the beauties of nature.

Burch (1965; 1969) reported two more conceptually-based studies during this early period. Both focused on camping activity in the Pacific Northwest. The former identified six types of play activity symbolic of the various meanings ascribed to camping. The latter tested two conventional theories of leisure behavior: the compensatory theory, suggesting that leisure activities are selected to be opposite to and give relief from routine activities, and the familiarity theory, suggesting that leisure activities are selected to be in conformance with routine activities to avoid feelings of uncertainty. Little support was found for either theory. Other studies of this early period (LaPage 1967; Catton 1969;

Shafer and Mietz 1969) were also exploratory and found diverse motivations for participation in camping and wilderness use.

A Behavioral Approach to Recreation

Beginning in the early 1970s Driver and associates began laying a conceptual foundation for the study of motivations in outdoor recreation (Driver and Toucher 1970; Driver and Brown 1975; Driver 1976; Driver and Brown 1978; Haas et al. 1980a).[1] They also developed an empirical approach to testing their concepts which has received wide application over the past decade. The conceptual foundation of their work began with a fundamental look at the nature of recreation (Driver and Toucher 1970), noting that the traditional view of recreation is based on activities—fishing, swimming, camping, etc. While this activity approach has been useful for a variety of descriptive purposes, it leaves unaddressed a number of potentially important issues:

> Why is the recreationist participating in the activity? What other activities might have been selected if the opportunities existed? What satisfactions or rewards are received from the activity? How can the quality of the experience be enhanced? (Driver and Toucher 1970, p. 10)

To better answer these analytical questions, a behavioral approach was proposed where recreation is defined as "an experience that results from recreational engagements" (Driver and Toucher 1970).

This approach is based on received psychological theory which suggests that most human behavior is goal-directed or aimed at some need satisfaction. Perhaps the most widely recognized expression of this theory is Maslow's (1943) hierarchy of human needs beginning with the most basic requirements for physiological sustenance and ranging through more aesthetic concerns. The work of Driver and associates is based more directly on expectancy theory developed in social psychology, which suggests that people engage in activities in specific settings to realize a group of psychological outcomes which are known, expected, and valued (e.g. Atkinson and Birch 1972; Lawler 1973; Fishbein and Ajzen 1974). Thus people select and participate in recreation activities to meet certain goals or satisfy certain needs, and recreation activities are more a means to an end than an end in themselves.

The behavioral approach has been expanded to recognize four levels or hierarchies of demand for outdoor recreation (Table 6-1) (Driver and Brown 1978; Haas et al. 1980a). Level 1 represents demands for activities themselves and has been the traditional focus of recreation research and planning. Level 2 represents the various settings in which activities take place. An activity such

---

[1] The experiences derived from participation in recreation activities have been subject to a variety of terminology including "motivations," "satisfactions," "psychological outcomes," and "experience expectations." The term "motivations" is used generally throughout this chapter for the sake of consistency.

as camping, for example, can be undertaken in a variety of environmental, social, and managerial settings, each representing different recreation opportunities. Level 2 demands do not exist in and of themselves; people participate in activities in different settings to realize experiences as represented by Level 3. These experiences are satisfactions, motivations, or desired psychological outcomes. Examples include enjoyment of the out-of-doors, applying and developing skills, strengthening family ties, learning, getting exercise, exploring, reflecting on personal values, temporarily escaping a variety of adverse stimuli at home or at work, taking risks, and so on. Typically, more than one experience is sought and realized from recreation participation. Finally, Level 4 demands refer to ultimate benefits which flow from satisfying experiences derived from recreation participation. These benefits may be either personal or societal, but are rather abstract and are difficult to measure and associate directly with recreational participation. For this reason empirical study of the behavioral approach to recreation has focused on Level 3 demands.[2]

A behavioral approach to recreation has been suggested by a number of other recreation researchers as well. Hendee (1974), for example, proposed what he termed a "multiple satisfaction approach" to hunting, expanding measures of satisfaction from the traditional count of game killed to include more varied motivations and satisfactions.

In a rudimentary sense, a behavioral approach to recreation was a basis for the major philosophical writing which characterized recreation literature of the 1950s and early 1960s. Several classical theories were postulated to explain general leisure behavior. Two theories, compensation and familiarity, were described in the preceding section. Others included surplus energy (leisure activity burns off excess energy or vitality), relaxation (leisure activity provides respite from intense work or living functions), and catharsis (leisure activity allows purging of emotional tension or anxiety). Standard works in this area include Neumeyer and Neumeyer (1949), Larrabee and Meyersohn (1958), Kaplan (1960), Brightbill (1960), and deGrazia (1962).

---

[2] This is not to say that the ultimate benefits of outdoor recreation participation have not received research attention. The results are simply not yet definitive enough to be used in management planning. A report for the Outdoor Recreation Resources Review Commission, for example, surveyed the literature on the relationship between outdoor recreation and mental health, concluding:

> Outdoor recreation can result in the kind of satisfying leisure behavior that is part of being mentally healthy. That does not mean that provision of outdoor recreation will produce mental health—and its absence, mental illness—but that the lives of a mentally healthy population will be improved by outdoor recreation, and that mentally ill people can also benefit from it (Gans 1962, p. 239).

West and Merriam (1970), Kaplan (1974), and Levitt (1982) are also representative of this genre of research.

A review by Levitt (1982) found approximately 100 studies on therapeutic aspects of camping for emotionally disturbed children and adolescents. While most of these studies have reported beneficial effects, consistent methodological weaknesses have limited their definitiveness.

Table 6-1.   Four levels or hierarchies of demand for outdoor recreation.

Level	Example 1	Example 2
1. Activities	Wilderness hiking	Family picnicking
2. Settings		
A. Environmental setting	Rugged terrain	Grass fields
B. Social setting	Few people	No boisterous teenagers
C. Managerial setting	No restrictions	Picnic tables
3. Experiences	Risk taking	In-group affiliation
	Challenge	Change of pace
	Physical exercise	
4. Benefits		
A. Personal	Enhanced self-esteem	Family solidarity
B. Societal	Increased commitment to conservation	Increased work production

Adapted from Haas et al. (1980a).

Empirical Tests of the Behavioral Approach

Empirical search for the motivations of general leisure behavior has occupied social scientists for a number of years and can be traced back as far as the 1920s with the classic Middletown studies of Lynd and Lynd (1929). Also representative of this early period was the study of Lundberg et al. (1934) which developed a list of eight reasons why high school students enjoyed their favorite leisure activity. But the research record is spotty until more recent times. Perhaps the first and best known of the more modern studies are those of Havighurst and associates. Donald and Havighurst (1959), for example, developed a twelve-item checklist of possible meanings of leisure activities, and found systematic relationships between these meanings and the activities in which subjects engaged.

Empirical studies of recreation motivations have flourished since the late 1960s. Though these studies share certain characteristics, they tend to fall into one of three general categories: studies of general leisure behavior, exploration of motivations for a specific activity, and the conceptual and empirical studies of Driver and associates.

The first and largest category is studies of general leisure behavior. While there are potentially important management implications involved in these studies (for example, the substitutability of leisure activities, addressed later in this chapter), their popularity has also been influenced by their heuristic value. Social scientists are generally intrigued by such studies as they allow exploration of why people behave as they do under conditions of few obvious constraints or compelling external forces. Several research approaches have been taken in this general category of studies:

1. Participation rates in various leisure activities have been used to group activities into similar categories (Bishop 1970; Moss and Lamphear 1970; Witt 1971; McKechnie 1974; Schmitz-Scherzer et al. 1974; Hendee and Burdge 1974; Ditton et al. 1975; Christensen and Yoesting 1977; London et al. 1977). Various numbers of activity categories which seem to share underlying meanings have been isolated.

2. Lists of potential motivations have been developed and tested for their importance in participation in leisure activities (Potter et al. 1973; Hollandar 1977; Rossman and Ulehla 1977; Tinsley et al. 1977; London et al. 1977; Hawes 1978; Tinsley and Kass 1978; Adams 1979; Crandall 1979; Tinsley and Kass 1979; Pierce 1980a; Beard and Ragheb 1980; Iso-Ahola and Allen 1982; Beard and Ragheb 1983). Various numbers of basic dimensions of leisure meanings have been isolated.

3. Perceived similarity of leisure activities has been used to group activities into similar categories (Ritchie 1975; Becker 1976). As in 1 above, various numbers of activity categories which seem to share underlying meanings have been isolated.

4. Antecedent or preceding conditions have been related to preferred leisure activity choice (Witt and Bishop 1970). Systematic relationships have been found indicating that certain leisure activities fulfill certain motivations created by antecedent conditions.

5. Personality traits of subjects have been related to participation in leisure activities (Moss et al. 1969; Moss and Lamphear 1970; Howard 1976) and more directly to motivations for participating in selected leisure activities (Driver and Knopf 1977). Systematic relationships have been found indicating that certain leisure activities fulfill certain motivations created by personality traits.

6. Attitudes toward leisure have been related to participation in leisure activities (Neulinger and Breit 1969; 1971). Systematic relationships have been found indicating that certain leisure activities fulfill certain motivations created by attitudes toward leisure.

7. Reported preferences for leisure activities have been used to group activities into similar categories (Hendee et al. 1971). Several activity categories have been isolated which seem to share underlying meanings.

8. Descriptions and characteristics of leisure activities have been rated and grouped into similar categories (Pierce 1980b; 1980c). Several categories of both descriptions and characteristics of leisure activities have been isolated which seem to share underlying meanings.

9. Participation rates in various leisure activities have been used to group participants into similar categories (Romsa 1973). Several groups of participants have been isolated based on similiarity of leisure activities.

Integration of these studies is difficult for several reasons. Leisure activities and motivations studied have varied widely, as have research approaches and sample populations. Moreover, the statistical methods used are commonly complex, multivariate data reduction techniques such as factor analysis, cluster

Table 6-2.   Leisure motivation categories and scale items.

1. *Enjoying nature, escaping civilization*
   To get away from civilization for awhile
   To be close to nature
2. *Escape from routine and responsibility*
   Change from my daily routine
   To get away from the responsibilities of
   my everyday life
3. *Physical exercise*
   For the exercise
   To help keep me in shape
4. *Creativity*
   To be creative
5. *Relaxation*
   To relax physically
   So my mind can slow down for awhile
6. *Social contact*
   So I could do things with my compan-
   ions
   To get away from other people
7. *Meeting new people*
   To talk to new and varied people
   To build friendships with new people
8. *Heterosexual contact*
   To be with people of the opposite sex
   To meet people of the opposite sex
9. *Family contact*
   To be away from the family for awhile
   To help bring the family together more

10. *Recognition, status*
    To show others I could do it
    So others would think highly of me
    for doing it
11. *Social power*
    To have control over others
    To be in a position of authority
12. *Altruism*
    To help others
13. *Stimulus seeking*
    For the excitement
    Because of the risks involved
14. *Self-actualization (feedback, self-
    improvement, ability utilization)*
    Seeing the results of my efforts
    Using a variety of skills and talents
15. *Achievement, challenge, competition*
    To develop my skills and ability
    Because of the competition
    To learn what I am capable of
16. *Killing time, avoiding boredom*
    To keep busy
    To avoid boredom
17. *Intellectual aestheticism*
    To use my mind
    To think about my personal values

From Crandall (1980)

analysis, multidimensional scaling, and discriminant analysis. These techniques are appropriate, but yield results requiring considerable interpretation by the researcher. Nevertheless, these studies as a whole do reveal that leisure activities have underlying meanings to participants, and that these underlying meanings or motivations can be empirically defined. Based on a recent review by Crandall (1980) a fairly discrete and comprehensive list of general leisure motivations has been developed and is shown, along with the scale items used to test these motivations, in Table 6-2.

A small and somewhat miscellaneous group of studies follows up on the early explorations described at the beginning of this chapter. All focus on specific outdoor recreation activities and either explore a limited number of potential motivations or use an open-ended question technique. Two studies, for example, surveyed fishermen, asking them to rank possible reasons for fishing (Moeller and Engelken 1972; Witter et al. 1982). Both studies gained some insight into motivations for fishing, particularly the existence of different motivations for different types of fishing. Management implications of this type of study are that different aspects of the fishing environment should be emphasized to enhance satisfaction for different types of fishermen.

A similar study of deer hunting was done by Decker et al. (1980) who found considerable diversity on the importance of various motivations for hunting. These findings support the multiple satisfactions approach of Hendee, demonstrating that hunters clearly ascribe more meaning to hunting than simply bagging game.[3]

Finally, Towler (1977) and Hendee et al. (1977) explored motivations of visitors to backcountry areas using an open-ended survey approach. Both studies found a variety of reported motivations. Hendee et al. (1977) found twelve primary reasons for visiting high mountain lakes, with no one reason reported by more than 29 percent of the sample. Towler (1977) found six general categories of motivations for hiking in Grand Canyon National Park, with motivations having a significant effect on visitor expectations for and attitudes about backcountry conditions.

Taken together, the studies in this category suggest that motivations for outdoor recreation—indeed, motivations even within a single outdoor recreation activity—are diverse and related to the attitudes, preferences, and expectations of users.

A large and growing group of studies is based directly on the conceptual and empirical work of Driver and associates. To test their conceptual formulations of a behavioral approach to recreation, these researchers have developed and refined a highly comprehensive list of potential recreation motivations, measured empirically by a series of scale items. Respondents are asked to rate the relative importance of each scale item representing a potential motivation for participating in a designated recreation activity. Scale items are usually then reduced through cluster analysis to "domains" representing more generalized categories of motivations. This basic research approach is similar to the studies

---

[3] While there are certainly multiple motivations and sources of satisfaction in hunting, the importance of bagging game should not be unduly minimized. An open-ended survey conducted by Stankey et al. (1973) asked respondents what big-game hunting means. A majority of hunters replied in terms of game bagging outcomes, though a substantial minority gave general outdoor enjoyment and environmental amenity responses. The authors conclude from their study:

Success [game-bagging] is only one outcome to which hunters aspire; satisfactions derived from esthetic enjoyment, solitude, sociability, challenge, and other aspects of the experience represent significant, and perhaps at times, superior returns to the individual (Stankey et al. 1973, p. 82).

It seems reasonable to conclude that some minimally acceptable chance of bagging game is a necessary but generally insufficient element of managing hunting, and other elements will also be necessary to ensure broadly satisfying hunting experiences.

cited in item 2 on page 83. Its potential usefulness for outdoor recreation managers is enhanced, however, because of its direct focus on outdoor recreation activities and its standardization as a result of extensive empirical testing. The motivation scales have been developed and refined through dozens of empirical studies, generating in excess of 20,000 useable questionnaires. Tests have generally confirmed both the reliability and validity of the motivation scales (Rosenthal et al. 1982).

The first generation of these studies was applied to a variety of recreation activities, but published results focused primarily on fishing (Knopf et al. 1973; Driver and Knopf 1976; Driver and Cooksey 1977) and river floating (Roggenbuck and Schreyer 1977; Schreyer and Roggenbuck 1978; Graefe et al. 1981; Knopf and Lime 1984). As in the 1982 study of Witter et al. discussed earlier, differences in motivations were found between types of fishermen. Trout fishermen, for instance, rated the motivation of "affiliation" substantially lower than did lake and bank fishermen.

Motivation scales have been included in a series of nationwide studies by Lime and associates investigating river floating (Knopf and Lime 1984). Their data illustrate the potential management implications of this research approach. Table 6-3 presents two examples. The first compares responses of river floaters on two rivers to seven motivations. Floaters on both rivers rated "view scenery" and "peace and calm" very highly, but differed substantially on other motivations. Floaters on the Delta River placed much more emphasis on learning, developing skills, exercise, escaping crowds, and being alone than did their counterparts on the Salt River. Though floaters on both rivers desired "peace and calm," they apparently define it in different ways. These findings are reminiscent of the different meanings of solitude and privacy in outdoor recreation discussed in Chapter Five. The implications of these findings translate directly into river management objectives, particularly with respect to appropriate contact levels.

The second example in Table 6-3 illustrates that even floaters on the same river can differ substantially on motivations. Both first-time and repeat

Table 6-3.   Motivations for river floating by percentage of respondents.

			Rio Grande River	
	Delta River	Salt River	First-time visitors	Repeat visitors
View scenery	97	77	88	94
Peace and calm	85	73	62	82
Learn new things	80	50	78	73
Develop skills	78	34	48	76
Escape crowds	76	30	52	82
Exercise	64	48	34	65
Be alone	28	8	6	22

Adapted from Knopf and Lime (1984)

visitors on the Rio Grande River, New Mexico, rated "view scenery," "peace and calm," and "learn new things" highly. But there were substantial differences between the two groups of floaters on the other four motivations, implying that repeat visitors had a substantially higher sensitivity to density. Unless this is taken into account in river management, many repeat visitors are likely to be dissatisfied and perhaps eventually displaced. The authors conclude that data of this kind illustrate the advantage of managing for recreation experiences rather than activities:

> It is clear that repeat visitors on the Rio Grande are looking for different experiences than first-time visitors. It is also clear that Delta River visitors differ in orientation from Salt River visitors. Yet, all four populations are participating in the same recreation activity, river floating. From an activity perspective, they would be viewed as essentially equivalent and not differing in resource requirements. But from an experience perspective, they would be viewed as distinct recreation populations with separate requirements (Knopf and Lime 1984, p. 15).

A study of floaters on the Green and Yampa Rivers, Dinosaur National Monument (Roggenbuck and Schreyer 1977; Schreyer and Roggenbuck 1978) illustrated that motivations for recreation are related to user attitudes, preferences, and perceptions of crowding. Selected motive domains were found to be related to a statistically significant degree with attitudes about maximum group size, preferences for campsite development, campsite assignment, trip scheduling, levels of encounters, and perceptions of crowding, though the correlations were not strong.

Graefe et al. (1981) compared the above findings with data from a similar study on the Rio Grande River, Big Bend National Park. Remarkable similarity was found between the studies with regard to some motivations. In particular, learning about and experiencing nature and stress release and solitude were the most important motivations across both samples and exhibited highly similar factor domain structures. But, as might be expected from samples drawn from rivers with substantially varying environmental, social, and managerial conditions, other motivational scale items and domains differed quite dramatically.

A second generation of studies has added another methodological step to identify types of recreationists based on motive structure. After appropriate motive domains have been isolated as described above, a further clustering procedure is used to identify groups of respondents having relatively homogeneous patterns of response to the motive domains. In this way similar groups or "market segments" of recreationists sharing similar motivations are identified. These studies have been conducted on hunters (Brown et al. 1977; Hautaluoma and Brown 1978; Hautaluoma et al. 1982), river floaters (Ditton et al. 1982), wilderness visitors (Brown and Haas 1980), ski tourers (Haas et al. 1980b), and visitors to an historical park (Knopf and Barnes 1980).

All of these studies were able to identify between three and ten groups of respondents with distinctive recreation motivations. Moreover, there were often relationships between the various types of recreationists identified and variables such as attitudes and preferences about management actions. The example of wilderness visitors will be used to illustrate this type of study.

Brown and Haas (1980) conducted a survey of 300 visitors to the Rawah Wilderness Area, Colorado, by mail and attained an 88 percent response rate. Initial cluster analysis identified eight motivational domains important across the sample (see Table 6-4). Respondents were then grouped through a second clustering procedure according to their scores on the eight motivational domains, and five types of visitors were thus identified.

The authors go on to describe each visitor type in more detail and to suggest ways in which this kind of information might be incorporated in wilderness management planning. For example, visitor types 1 and 2 both place moderate to strong positive emphasis on seven of the eight motivational domains, but differ on the eighth, Meeting/Observing Other People. Type 1 visitors (19 percent of the sample) rated this domain as slightly adding to satisfaction, while type 2 visitors (10 percent of the sample) rated this domain as moderately detracting from satisfaction. These findings have obvious management implications in that two wilderness zones might be created serving somewhat different objectives and visitors. Both zones would be managed to serve the first seven motivations described (Closeness to Nature, Escape Pressure, etc.) but with different use densities and contact levels allowed.

Empirical tests, then, have generally supported a behavioral approach to recreation. People participate in recreation activities to fulfill a variety of motivations, and these motivations are identifiable empirically. By grouping recreationists into similar types based on motivations, recreation areas can potentially be planned and managed more directly for a variety of satisfying experiences.

Expanding the Behavioral Approach

The behavioral approach to outdoor recreation has been applied by a number of researchers to enhance understanding of several other recreation management issues, including the substitutability of recreation activities, the causes of conflict between recreationists, and linkages between motivations for recreation and attributes of outdoor recreation settings.

Substitutability. Several studies in the early 1970s explored the issue of substitutability of recreation activities (Moss and Lamphear 1970; Hendee and Burdge 1974; O'Leary et al. 1974). They postulated that if the underlying meaning of recreation activities could be discovered, activities sharing the same meanings might be substituted for one another. The management implications of this issue are potentially large, particularly in terms of economic efficiency: if

Table 6-4. Five types of visitors to the Rawah Wilderness Area, Colorado.

Type	Number of respondents[a]	Percent of sample	Motivational Domain							
			Relationship with nature	Escape pressures	Autonomy	Achievement	Reflection on personal values	Sharing/recollection	Risk taking	Meeting/observing other people
1	50	19	Most strongly added[b]	Most strongly added	Strongly added	Strongly added	Strongly added	Strongly added	Slightly added	Slightly added
2	27	10	Most strongly added	Strongly added	Strongly added	Strongly added	Strongly added	Moderately added	Slightly added	Moderately detracted
3	44	17	Strongly added	Strongly added	Moderately added	Strongly added	Moderately added	Strongly added	Neither	Slightly added
4	53	20	Strongly added	Strongly added	Strongly added	Moderately added	Moderately added	Slightly added	Slightly added	Neither
5	60	23	Moderately added	Moderately added	Moderately added	Slightly added	Slightly added	Slightly added	Neither	Neither

Adapted from Brown and Haas (1980).

a Thirty respondents (11 percent of the sample) were identified as unique in the sense they were not grouped with any of the five types. This was primarily a function of missing data for these respondents rather than some true uniqueness.

b Respondents were asked to state the importance of these motivations to their satisfaction.

lower cost activities (e.g., pool swimming) could be substituted for higher cost activities (e.g., coastal swimming), substantial savings could be realized without a loss in participant satisfaction.

The early studies in this area clustered recreation activities together based on participation rates of respondents (Moss and Lamphear 1970; Hendee and Burdge 1974). It was suggested that since participation in activities within clusters was highly intercorrelated, activities within the same cluster may provide similar satisfactions and thus be substitutable. It was noted, however, that this aproach was "suggestive rather than conclusive" (Hendee and Burdge 1974). Christensen and Yoesting (1977) asked respondents directly if they could substitute activities in the same cluster without loss of satisfaction. A range of 45 to 67 percent of respondents across four activity clusters studied reported they could substitute activities without loss of satisfaction. However, the large number of respondents who could not substitute activities within the same cluster indicated that the issue of substitutability is more complex than first conceptualized. This may be a function of the methods used to study substitutability: factor or cluster analysis of recreation activities based on participation rates may group activities that are complimentary (or similar in meaning) rather than truly substitutable (or nearly identical in meaning) (Beaman 1975).

Two studies have attempted to develop insights into substitutability based more directly on motivations. Tinsley and Johnson (1984) developed a preliminary taxonomy of leisure activities by measuring the motivations respondents associated with them. Nine relatively homogeneous groups of activities were identified that appear to satisfy similar motivations. Activities within the same group might then be substitutable. Baumgartner and Heberlein (1981) surveyed goose and deer hunters in Wisconsin to determine perceived substitutes for these activities. Deer hunters reported substantially fewer substitutes than goose hunters, as well as higher mean ratings on items measuring the importance of social interaction with hunting party members, socialization in the activity, and selected goals or meanings of the activity. Apparently, the underlying meanings of the activity, including the strength with which they are held, affect the degree to which recreation activities are substitutable.

Potential usefulness of the substitutability concept in recreation management has been limited by the small base of empirical research. Preliminary findings, however, indicate that underlying motivations for recreation are instrumental in determining which activities are substitutable. More research is needed before the management implications of the substitutability concept can be realized.

Recreation Conflict. As noted in Chapter Five, studies of conflict between people participating in different recreation activities are legion. Conflicts have been found between fishermen and canoeists, fishermen and water skiers, snowmobilers and ski tourers, motorbike riders and hikers, to list a few. Several recent studies have attempted to go beyond documentation of such conflicts and discover why they exist. The principal conceptual foundation of these studies is the theory of goal interference: conflict results when the behavior of one group of recreationists is incompatible with the social, psychological, or physical goals of another group (Jacob and Schreyer 1980; Gramann and Burdge 1981). The theory is rooted in the goal-oriented view of human behavior described early in this chapter and has been widely adopted in general conflict research (Sargent 1967; Sawrey 1970; Sawrey and Telford 1975). Substantial evidence has accumulated in support of this view, especially with regard to differences in recreation motivation.

Driver and associates found early evidence of recreation conflict as a function of motivations (Knopf et al. 1973; Driver and Bassett 1975). Their initial studies of motivations for recreation over twelve activities included both fishermen and canoeists on the conflict-plagued Au Sable River, Michigan. Fishermen scored the lowest of any study group on the motivation of affiliation, while canoeists scored nearly the highest. Perhaps these fundamental differences in motivations might explain the classic conflict between these two activities.

Gramann and Burdge (1981) found additional evidence for this view in a study of fishermen and water skiers on a reservoir in Illinois. Fishermen were divided into two groups: those considered to have experienced conflict (defined as observing reckless boating), and those considered not to have experienced conflict. Significant differences were found between the two groups on several intuitively meaningful motivations including escape, enjoying the smells and sounds of nature, using and discussing equipment, feeling their independence, doing things with their familiy, and chancing dangerous situations. The differences, however, were rather weak statistically, though this may have been due to the indirect measure of conflict.

Jackson and Wong's (1982) study is also supportive of the notion that conflict is related to differences in recreation motivations. Cross-country skiers and snowmobilers in Alberta, Canada, were surveyed as to their recreational orientation (as expressed by their participation in other recreation activities) and motivations for participation. Significant differences were found between the two groups on both aspects. The characteristics of the two activities studied were found to carry over into other recreational activities. Snowmobilers tended to participate in more extractive, active, and mechanized activities, while cross-country skiers tended to participate in passive, self-propelled, and low-impact activities. Moreover, there were statistically significant differences between the two groups on eleven of the sixteen motivation items studied. The authors conclude:

> Perceived motivational conflicts are best understood not simply as an outcome of the choice of activity, but rather as stemming from a fundamental orientation of recreational preferences, expressed conceptually in terms of participation in other activities, and motivations for participation (Jackson and Wong 1982, p. 59).

The evidence reviewed above strongly suggests that motivations play an important role in determining recreation conflict and that conflicts might be alleviated by grouping recreationists according to similar motivations.

Linking Motives, Settings, and Activities. The behavioral approach to outdoor recreation suggests not only that people participate in recreation to fulfill certain motivations, but also that fulfillment of these motivations is dependent upon both the settings in which participation occurs and the activities in which participants engage. In other words, there are linkages between the hierarchies or levels of demand for outdoor recreation described early in this chapter (see Table 6-1). Identification of these linkages would be of considerable assistance to managers, for managers cannot fulfill the motivations of visitors directly. Rather, they create opportunities to fulfill motives by manipulating the recreation setting and activities available. This approach to outdoor recreation management has been termed "experience-based setting management" (Driver and Rosenthal 1982; Manfredo et al. 1983).

Relationships between motives, settings, and activities have received little empirical testing.[4] Some of these linkages appear intuitively obvious. Opportunities for contact with the natural environment, for example, are likely to be enhanced through limited development of the setting. Opportunities to get away from others will be enhanced in relatively low-density use areas. And opportunities for challenge and risk-taking should be greater in areas providing only low-standard trails and other improvements. But these are only generalities and knowledge about such relationships would be increased by empirical testing.

Several recent studies have begun searching for these relationships. Haas et al. (1979) studied both motivations and physical setting preferences of visitors to three western wilderness areas. Respondents reacted to a series of scaled items for both motivations and physical setting attributes and these response sets were cluster analyzed following the procedures developed by Driver and associates. Several domains for both motivations and setting attributes were identified, but no attempt was made to relate the two. Brown and Ross (1982) attempted to go a step further in a study of visitors to the Glenwood Springs Resource Area, Colorado. Multiple regression analysis was used to explore for relationships between motivations and settings and a number of such relationships were found. The statistical significance of these relationships was generally enhanced when the sample was grouped according to activity. In other words, people sharing the same activity have more uniform relationships between motivations and setting preferences than all recreationists considered together.

---

[4] It should be noted, however, that several studies described early in this chapter found relationships between motivations for recreation and attitudes about management actions which are suggestive of linkages between motives, settings, and activities.

Two groups of researchers have conducted more thorough tests of these relationships. McLaughlin and Paradice (1980) surveyed snowmobilers and cross-country skiers asking them to rate motivation scale items and scale items describing selected attributes of the physical, social, and management environments. Cluster analysis revealed four basic types of visitors based on recreation motivations. A number of statistical relationships were found between these types of users and desired attributes of the recreation environment. Manfredo et al. (1983) surveyed visitors to three wilderness areas, asking respondents to rate a number of motivation, setting attribute, and management action scale items. Each set of scale items was cluster analyzed and five of the motivation clusters were selected for further object cluster analysis, isolating three visitor types based on similar motivation ratings. Type 1 visitors were labeled the High Risk/Achievement Group, type 2 visitors were labeled the Low Risk/Social Interaction Group, and type 3 visitors, who represented the largest proportion of all visitors (60 percent of the sample) and tended to be less distinctive in their motivation ratings, were labeled the Norm Group. The three types of visitors were then examined to see if there were significant differences between them in activities engaged in and preferences for setting attributes and management actions. A number of differences were found.

Though there were no differences among the three groups with regard to the four activities having the highest participation rates and the one activity with a very low participation rate, there were differences for the two activities with moderate participation rates. In addition, there were statistically significant differences between the three types of visitors on seven of the setting attribute clusters and four of the management action clusters. Though the magnitude of the differences was generally not large, it must be remembered that the sample was relatively homogeneous—all respondents were wilderness visitors—and a more diverse respondent group would likely yield greater levels of statistical significance. The authors go on in their report to suggest ways in which these findings might be incorporated directly into management objectives and prescriptions.

Two other studies have used different but less direct approaches to linking motives, settings, and activities. The first approach has been an effort to translate motivational scale items directly into management terms (Knopp et al. 1979). Respondents were asked to rate a series of environmental setting elements which were designed to reflect basic motivations, rather than motivational items themselves. The data set was combined with preferences for eleven management actions and reduced through cluster analysis to four rather distinct associations, descriptively labeled "noise and development tolerant," "activity setting," "nature and solitude," and "nature with comfort and security." The second approach studied motivations for river floating across eleven diverse rivers (Knopf et al. 1983). The study hypothesized that if motives are related to setting attributes then significant differences in motives should be found across diverse settings. The results were mixed. While some significant differences in motives were found, there was a striking general similarity of motives. However, the degree to which similar motives were satisfied in different settings was not addressed.

It is clear that linkages between motives, settings, and activities as postulated by the behavioral approach to outdoor recreation are far from being definitively established, though the preliminary evidence gathered thus far tends to support the concept of such linkages. Much more empirical research will be needed, though, before these linkages can be incorporated directly into management planning.

Measuring Motives: Methodological Issues

While there are a number of issues inherent in measuring motivations for recreation, one in particular seems fundamental yet has received little attention. This concerns the basic measurement approach or technique. It was noted in Chapter Five that the search for relationships between density and crowding has been partially confounded by the measurement techniques used: attitude surveys and behavioral observations have sometimes yielded conflicting results. Confidence in the findings of social science research can be considerably bolstered when similar results are obtained from divergent study approaches.

Driver (1976) has noted that there are three basic approaches to measuring human behavior in general, and motivations for recreation in particular: verbal behavior, overt nonverbal behavior, and physiological response. Each approach has inherent strengths and weaknesses and each approach should ideally be used as a check on the others. However, as with crowding research, nearly all studies on motivations for recreation have relied on verbal behavior as manifested in written responses to attitude surveys. Exceptions include a study by Bryan (1977) which relied at least partially on participant observation and studies of pupillary response to natural landscape scenes (Wenger and Videbeck 1969; Peterson and Neumann 1969), though these studies had little focus on motivations for recreation. Additional attention to alternative measures of motivations will enhance the confidence with which findings might be applied in the field.

An additional methodological issue is the time and location at which motivations are measured. A study of the visitor motivation for escaping physical stress was administered to fishermen both on-site and four months later by mail (Manfredo 1984). Inconsistencies were found in responses among the same group of subjects. As in the discussion of methodological issues in Chapter Five, there is little to indicate which measurement approach is "better." The key seems to be consistency so as to allow comparisons between areas or over time.

Summary and Conclusions

1. *Interpretation of outdoor recreation has evolved from an "activity approach" to a "behavioral approach" which focuses on why people participate in recreation activities and the experiences gained from such participation.*

2. *An expanded view of the behavioral approach recognizes four levels of demand for outdoor recreation: activities, settings, experiences, and benefits.*

3. *Empirical tests of the behavioral approach to outdoor recreation indicate that there are a variety of motivations for participating in outdoor recreation and these motivations can be empirically identified.*

4. *Outdoor recreationists can be segmented into relatively homogeneous groups based on their motivations.*

5. *Preliminary data suggest there are relationships between motivations for outdoor recreation and the settings and activities engaged in, though these relationships are not well developed.*

6. *Closer definition of the relationships between motivations, settings, and activities may enhance the degree to which outdoor recreation management can provide satisfying recreation experiences.*

7. *Substitutability of outdoor recreation activities is an issue with potentially important management implications, but is currently not well understood. Preliminary data, however, suggest that motivations may be instrumental in determining which activities are substitutable.*

8. *Incompatible motivations for outdoor recreation are an important contributor to conflicts between recreationists and recreation activities.*

9. *Alternative techniques should be applied to measuring recreation motivations to provide methodological checks on the predominate verbal/attitudinal approach.*

Chapter Seven

The Recreation Opportunity Spectrum: Designs for Diversity

Diversity in Outdoor Recreation

Over the course of this book numerous studies of visitors to outdoor recreation areas have been reviewed. The objectives, scope, and methods of these studies have been highly variable, but at least one general conclusion has been forthcoming: public tastes for outdoor recreation are diverse. This has been a recurring theme whether in regard to socio-economic and cultural characteristics (Chapter Two), attitudes about policy, and preferences for services and facilities (Chapter Three), desired contact level (Chapter Five), or motivation for recreation participation (Chapter Six). Diversity in tastes is found equally in early studies of developed campgrounds and more recent investigations of wilderness hikers. King, for example, in an early study of users at automobile campgrounds concluded that the data:

> . . . illustrate the characteristic heterogeneity of camping as a recreation activity and the multitude of reasons people may have for camping. Diversity in the kinds of facilities provided is an important consideration in recreation planning (King 1966, p. 2).

A more recent study of wilderness visitors concludes similarly:

> Wilderness visitors are not in any sense a uniform or homogeneous population . . . Represented among wilderness visitors are value systems that cover a wide and often conflicting range (Stankey 1972, p. 92).

Burch (1966) points out that not only are there differences in taste between people, but also that people's tastes change over time. A study in the Pacific Northwest found that the type of camping chosen (wilderness camping, automobile camping, or some combination of the two) was strongly related to changes in stage of the family life cycle. A nationwide panel study of campers found similar relationships between camping activity and family life cycle (LaPage 1973; LaPage and Ragain 1974). Based on these relationships, Burch concluded that "The forest camping system is like an omnibus—the seats are often full but often occupied by different persons as they adjust to the flow of time" (Burch 1966).

Diversity is also evident when the averaging issue in outdoor recreation is recognized. Shafer's (1969) "average camper who doesn't exist" was described in Chapter Three. Wagar (1966) seized on this issue, using the example of camping facilities. He pointed out that some campers prefer very elaborate facilities for comfort and convenience, while others prefer relatively simple facilities. Moreover, there is a wide range of opinion between these extremes. Providing a single, uniform type of camping opportunity—near the midpoint of the range based on averages, indeed at *any* point along the range—will leave many campers, quite possibly even the majority, less than fully satisfied. However, by offering a range of possibilities more campers' preferences can be met.

Wagar continued this line of reasoning to arrive at a definition of quality in outdoor recreation based on diversity. The difficulty of distinguishing between quality and type of recreation opportunities has plagued both visitors and managers. It is common to associate certain types of recreation opportunities with high quality quite subjectively. Those whose recreation tastes are oriented toward the remote and primitive, for example, probably consider wilderness recreation to be of high quality and automobile campgrounds as something less. But high quality can (and should) be found among all types of recreation opportunities. In this context, quality is properly defined as the degree to which a recreation opportunity meets the needs of those who seek it. Thus, from a broad management perspective, quality in outdoor recreation is equated with provision of diverse recreation opportunities.

Diversity has also been rationalized in economic terms. Wagar (1974) illustrates this, using a hypothetical undeveloped recreation area. If the area were to be used for wilderness recreation, it might support 3,000 user-days of recreation each year. If intensively developed, it might support 300,000 user-days of recreation. But the decision between these two alternatives should take into account the issue of scarcity. If developed recreation opportunities are relatively plentiful, and wilderness recreation scarce, society may place more value on creating additional wilderness recreation opportunities even though they will accommodate fewer user-days. This is in keeping with the economic theory of marginal utility: the more we have of some good or value, the less importance is placed on each additional unit. This rationale has been borne out in an empirical test of Colorado deer hunting (Miller et al. 1977) which explored willingness to pay for selected types of hunting opportunities. The value of deer hunting was found to vary among types of hunting opportunities and types of hunting groups. From this, it was demonstrated that total satisfaction of hunters (as measured by willingness to pay) could be increased by providing diversity in hunting opportunities.

Diversity has also been rationalized in political terms. Burch (1974) argues that without broad political support outdoor recreation areas are not likely to be maintained by society at large, and that this support is not likely to be forthcoming if outdoor recreation areas do not serve the needs of many. Managers should therefore strive to serve this diversity and not adhere too closely to any one group's ideas. Writing in the context of wilderness, and what he feels is an unacceptably narrow interpretation of wilderness, Burch concludes:

If we insist that wilderness is an island entire of itself, a sacred thing set above and beyond the political life of man, then, like all false idols, it will deserve its fate. And we shall all be equally diminished (Burch 1974, pp. 100-101).

Designs for Diversity

Several writers have noted that a systems approach to outdoor recreation management is needed if diversity is to be designed appropriately. It would be difficult for a single recreation area, regardless of size, to provide a full spectrum of opportunities. Examining each recreation area in isolation will usually lead to management decisions favoring the majority or plurality of potential visitors. While this is justified in many cases, the process will generally result in an entire system of recreation areas designed for the average visitor while neglecting a desirable element of diversity. Instead, each recreation area should be evaluated as part of a system of areas, each contributing as best it can to serve the diverse needs of the public. In this way, low density and other minority recreation opportunities can be justified (Wagar 1974). Stankey (1974) endorses this approach and suggests it best be applied on a regional basis, concluding that this is the best manner in which management can ensure "a diverse resource base capable of providing a variety of satisfactions."

Recognition of the need for diversity has led to a number of suggested classification or zoning systems for recreation areas. One of the earliest was contained in Carhart's (1961) handbook on wildland planning which suggested seven zones ranging from "wilderness" to "semi-suburban." The innovativeness of this concept is evident in his defense of the suggestion:

> To argue that "wilderness" can be anything less than physically "virgin" may be heresy. If so, I am a heretic. I do not argue that there can be any gradations of virginity. I do argue that there may be gradations in the physical attributes representing the wildness of wildlands, which as in other areas of human experience, may be as gratifying to those associating with it as absolute virginity—perhaps even more so (Carhart 1961, p. 69).

Just a year later the Outdoor Recreation Resources Review Commission (ORRRC 1962) included among its major recommendations a proposal for a six-fold classification system, ranging from high-density use to extensive primitive areas, to be applied to all federal recreation lands. A number of other recreation classification systems have been proposed (see Table 7-1). Recent attention, however, has focused on a relatively highly-developed recreation classification system called the Recreation Opportunity Spectrum (ROS).

Table 7-1.   Recreation classification or zoning systems.

Carhart (1961)	Seven wildland zones ranging from wilderness to semi-suburban
ORRRC (1962)	Six area classifications ranging from high-density to historic/cultural
National Park Service	Three area classifications: natural, historic, and recreational
U.S. Forest Service	Five recreation experience levels ranging from those emphasizing challenge, solitude, and demanding high skills to those involving extensive facilities and few skills.
Wild and Scenic Rivers Act (PL 90-542)	Three classes of rivers: wild, scenic, and recreational
National Trails Act (PL90-543)	Three classes of trails: scenic, recreational, and side.

The Recreation Opportunity Spectrum

ROS is a conceptual framework for encouraging diversity in outdoor recreation opportunities. A range of factors which define recreation opportunities are combined in alternative arrangements to describe diverse recreation experiences. But, as noted above, the concept of diversity underlying ROS is not new. Bultena and Klessig (1969), in their early conceptualization of satisfaction in camping, suggested components of camping they believed to be important to satisfaction, and referred to each of these components as "continua," a term which is at the heart of the ROS system. Similarly, Lloyd and Fischer (1972) recommended a continuum of recreation opportunities based on a range of six factors.

The distinguishing characteristic of ROS is the degree to which it has been formalized and translated into management guidelines. The relationships between site factors which combine to define recreation opportunities have been arranged in configurations which suggest categories of opportunities. Moreover, the system has been adopted by two major federal recreation agencies, the Forest Service and the Bureau of Land Management. ROS was developed simultaneously by two groups of researchers: Clark and Stankey (1979a) and Brown, Driver, and associates (Brown et al. 1978; Driver and Brown 1978; Brown et al. 1979). The approaches are quite similar, but some important differences also exist.

Both approaches to ROS recognize a four-fold hierarchical framework of demands for recreation as described in the previous chapter—activities, settings, psychological outcomes, and ultimate benefits—and the focus of both approaches is on Level 2 demands, settings. Brown, Driver, and associates take a more empirically-oriented approach to ROS, seeking to link settings to the motivations or psychological outcomes they fulfill. This is, of course, a natural extension of their work on motivations for recreation described in the previous chapter.

Clark and Stankey take a more applied approach. They note that as knowledge of linkages between recreation settings and psychological outcomes improves, so will the efficacy of meeting visitor demands. But in the meantime, managers should emphasize the provision of diversity in settings based on the assumption that a corresponding diversity of outcomes will be produced.

Both approaches also recognize, as discussed in Chapter Four, that recreation settings are defined by three broad categories of factors: environmental, social, and managerial. By describing ranges of these factors, selected types of recreation opportunity can be defined quite closely. Clark and Stankey (1979a) are most specific in defining these factors and the resulting recreation opportunity types. They suggest that six basic factors be used to define the opportunity spectrum; see Figure 7-1. Each opportunity type is defined by the combination of factors lying vertically beneath it in the figure.

Brown et al. (1978) take a more descriptive approach to defining opportunity types. Six opportunity classes are identified, as shown in Table 7-2. For each opportunity class, the associated experience provided, and the physical, social, and managerial settings are described.

In the broadest sense, ROS, like carrying capacity in Chapter Four, is a conceptual or organizing framework for thinking about recreation opportunities. It explicitly recognizes that experiences derived from recreation are related to the settings in which they occur, and that settings are a function of environmental, social, and managerial factors. By describing ranges of these factors, ROS illustrates the potential diversity of recreation opportunities.

ROS can be used in several ways, perhaps most importantly as an allocation and planning tool. Taking into account demands for recreation opportunities and their relative abundance, ROS can help guide allocation decisions so that each recreation area contributes to the diversity desirable in a complete system of recreation opportunities. Moreover, once an appropriate opportunity type has been chosen, ROS can help define specific management objectives for each setting attribute. Using noise as an example, Clark and Stankey (1979b) illustrate how ROS can be helpful in setting an appropriate management objective and ensuring that limits of acceptable change are not exceeded.

The specific setting attributes of ROS can be useful in designing and conducting inventories of recreation opportunities. ROS also provides an explicit framework within which consequences of alternative management actions can be evaluated. And, finally, ROS provides a means of matching

Text continues on page 105

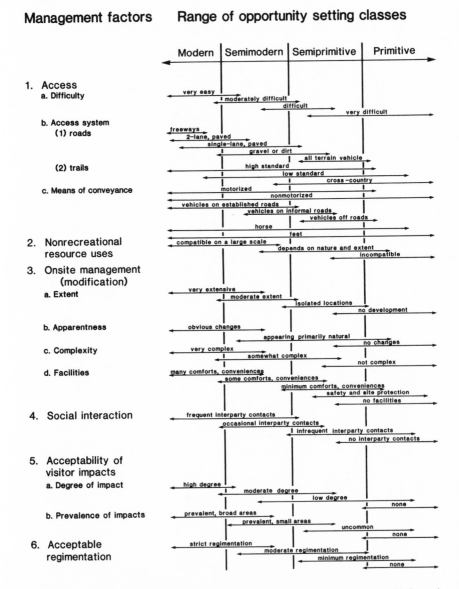

Figure 7-1.   Factors defining outdoor recreation opportunity settings. (Adapted from Clark and Stankey 1979)

Table 7-2.   The Recreation Opportunity Spectrum

Opportunity class	Experience opportunity	Physical, social, and managerial setting
Primitive (P)	Opportunity for isolation (from the sights and sounds of man), to feel a part of the natural environment, to have a high degree of challenge and risk, and to use outdoor skills.	Area is characterized by essentially unmodified natural environment of fairly large size. Concentration of users is very low and evidence of other area users is minimal. The area is managed to be essentially free from evidence of man-induced restrictions and controls. Only essential facilities for resource protection are used and are constructed of on-site materials. No facilities for comfort or convenience of the user are provided. Spacing of groups is informal and dispersed to minimize contacts with other groups or individuals. Motorized use within the area is not permitted.
Semi-primitive non-motorized (SPNM)	Some opportunity for isolation from the sight and sounds of man, but not as important as for primitive opportunities. Opportunity to have a high degree of interaction with the natural environment, to have moderate challenge and risk, and to use outdoor skills.	Area is characterized by a predominantly unmodified natural environment of moderate to large size. Concentration of users is low, but there is often evidence of other area users. The area is managed in such a way that minimum on-site controls and restrictions may be present, but are subtle. Facilities are primarily provided for the protection of resource values and safety of users. On-site materials are used where possible. Spacing of groups may be formalized to disperse use and provide low-to-moderate contacts with other groups or individuals. Motorized use is not permitted.
Semi-primitive motorized (SPM)	Some opportunity for isolation from the sights and sounds of man, but not as important as for primitive opportunities. Opportunity to have a high degree of interaction with the natural environment, to have moderate challenge and risk, and to use outdoor skills. Explicit opportunity to use motorized equipment while in the area.	Area is characterized by a predominantly unmodified natural environment of moderate to large size. Concentration of users is low, but there is often evidence of other area users. The area is managed in such a way that minimum on-site controls and restrictions may be present, but are subtle. Facilities are primarily provided for the protection of resource values and safety of users. On-site materials are used where possible. Spacing of groups may be formalized to disperse use and provide low-to-moderate contacts with other groups or individuals. Motorized use is permitted.

Continued on page 104

Table 7-2.   The Recreation Opportunity Spectrum (Cont.)

Opportunity class	Experience opportunity	Physical, social, and managerial setting
Rustic (R)	About equal opportunities for affiliation with user groups and opportunities for isolation from sights and sounds of man. Opportunity to have a high degree of interaction with the natural environment. Challenge and risk opportunities are not very important. Practice and testing of outdoor skills may be important. Opportunities for both motorized and nonmotorized forms of recreation are possible.	Area is characterized by predominantly natural environment with moderate evidences of the sights and sounds of man. Such evidences usually harmonize with the natural environment. Concentration of users may be low to moderate with facilities sometimes provided for group activity. Evidence of other users is prevalent. Controls and regimentation offer a sense of security and are on-site. Rustic facilities are provided for convenience of the user as well as for safety and resource protection. Moderate densities of groups is provided for in developed sites and on roads and trails. Low to moderate densities prevail away from developed sites and facilities. Renewable resource modification and utilization practices are evident, but harmonize with the natural environment. Conventional motorized use is provided for in construction standards and design of facilities.
Concentrated (C)	Opportunities to experience affiliation with individuals and groups are prevalent as is the convenience of sites and opportunities. These factors are generally more important than the setting of the physical environment. Opportunities for wildland challenges, risk taking, and testing of outdoor skills are unimportant, except for those activities like downhill skiing for which challenge and risk taking are important.	Area is characterized by substantially modified natural environment. Renewable resource modification and utilization practices are primarily to enhance specific recreation activities and to maintain vegetative cover and soil. Sights and sounds of man are readily evident, and the concentration of users is often moderate to high. A considerable number of facilities are designed for use by a large number of people. Facilities are often provided for special activities. Moderate to high densities of groups and individuals are provided for in developed sites, on roads and trails, and water surfaces. Moderate densities are provided for away from developed sites. Facilities for intensified motorized use and parking are available.

Table 7-2.   The Recreation Opportunity Spectrum (Cont.)

Opportunity class	Experience opportunity	Physical, social, and managerial setting
Modern urbanized (MU)	Opportunities to experience affiliation with individuals and groups are prevalent as is the convenience of sites and opportunities. These factors are more important than the setting of the physical environment. Opportunities for wildland challenges, risk taking, and testing outdoor skills are unimportant.	Area is characterized by a substantially urbanized environment, although the background may have natural elements. Renewable resource modification and utilization practices are to enhance specific recreation activities. Vegetative cover is often exotic and manicured. Soil protection usually accomplished with hard surfacing and terracing. Sights and sounds of man, on-site, are predominant. Large numbers of users can be expected both on-site and in nearby areas. A considerable number of facilities are designed for the use and convenience of large numbers of people and include electrical hookups and contemporary sanitation services. Controls and regimentation are obvious and numerous. Facilities for highly intensified motor uses and parking are available with forms of mass transit often available to carry people throughout the site.

From Brown et al. (1978)

desired visitor experiences with available opportunities. ROS provides relatively specific descriptions of available recreation opportunities so that visitors can more readily identify those opportunities likely to meet their desired experiences. Jubenville and Becker (1983) emphasize the desirability of this management approach. If recreation resources are consistently managed for a defined opportunity type which is made known to the public, this is likely to have substantial benefits to both visitors and managers. Visitors are more likely to be satisfied with the opportunities they find and managers are less likely to have to resort to regulatory measures designed to control inappropriate visitor use.

Extending the Opportunity Spectrum

ROS has received broad and deserved attention from both managers and researchers. As a relatively new concept, though, it can be expected to undergo some refinements in content and interpretation. The need for extended work on ROS has been explicitly noted by one of its original designers:

It is critical that current and potential users recognize that, although considerable research and management experience underlies the ROS, many judgments have been made in making it operational . . . The result is a "best guess" tool for planning, management, and research that will improve with experience if, and only if, the underlying assumptions, objectives and expectations, and documentations of its use are explicitly stated. Changes in the specifications of the ROS details *will be necessary* (Clark 1982, p. 10, emphasis in original).

One suggestion to extend ROS concerns the relationship between the three basic factors that describe recreation settings: environmental, social, and managerial conditions (Manning 1985). In ROS the implicit relationship between these factors is linear as shown in Figure 7-2. As environmental conditions change from natural to unnatural, social and managerial conditions change in a corresponding manner. As a result, only certain combinations of factors appear possible. Of course, the linear relationships suggested in ROS are intuitively meaningful in many, perhaps most, cases but theoretically, at least, there is no reason that natural environments cannot, or should not, support relatively high-density use under highly developed conditions. Moreover, there is empirical evidence to suggest demand for these and other unconventional recreation opportunities. The diversity of attitudes, preferences, and motivations of users discussed in earlier chapters is generally suggestive of this, and several studies have addressed this issue directly. Bultena and Taves (1961), for example, in an early study of the Quetico-Superior Area, Minnesota, found numerous "inconsistencies" among the response patterns of visitors. Noting that 99 percent of visitors strongly favored preserving the area in its natural state, the authors go on to point out that " . . . a relatively high proportion of the campers, and a somewhat smaller, although sizable proportion of the canoeists, inconsistently also favor the development of more facilities in the area" (Bultena and Taves 1961). The authors refer to this substantial subpopulation of users as "wilderness compromisers." A more recent study of the motivations of river users (Knopp et al. 1979) found that motivations tended to cluster into sets or packages, and that:

Most of the sets or packages . . . meet the criterion of conventional wisdom, or an intuitive notion of what belongs together. On occasion, however, a grouping may occur which appears incongruous to the manager or planner. This package may have a small but real constituency which deserves attention (Knopp et al. 1979, p. 325).

Potential users of ROS should be made explicitly aware of the wide ranging ways in which environmental, social, and managerial factors can be combined to produce diverse recreation opportunities. This seems in keeping with the intentions of the designers of ROS; publications describing the concept emphasize the need for diversity and caution that the guidelines offered to illustrate ROS, such as those contained in Figure 7-1, not be interpreted too strictly.

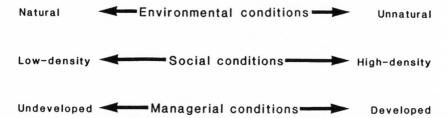

Figure 7-2. Linear relationship between environmental, social, and managerial conditions as suggested by ROS. (From Manning 1985)

There are indications, though, that ROS is being interpreted and applied rather rigidly. A recent article, for example, states that ROS works "by combining mixes of activities, settings, and experiences into six classes" and that "each acre or hectare of land and water in a planning area is put into one of the classes" (Buist and Hoots 1982).

A second issue concerning ROS is the extent to which recreation motivations can be directly linked with opportunity settings. The difficulty in defining these linkages was described in Chapter Six. Considering the inherent diversity in recreation motivations and settings, it seems unlikely that comprehensive, definitive guidelines could be developed which outline combinations of setting attributes which will fulfill selected motivations. The issue is further compounded by the apparent adaptability of people to recreation environments. The research on motivations in Chapter Six indicates that a recreation activity can fulfill more than one motivation and vice versa.

Driver and Brown (1984) suggest this basic limitation of ROS by pointing out that in the most fundamental sense it is visitors who produce recreation experiences and opportunities, not managers. Managers contribute to this process by providing what they believe to be appropriate settings. In view of these limitations, ROS might best be considered an organizing or conceptual framework like carrying capacity. As with carrying capacity, a considerable amount of management judgment will be needed.

Summary and Conclusions

1. There is great diversity in public tastes for outdoor recreation.
2. High quality can and should be found among all types of outdoor recreation.
3. For the individual, quality is defined as the degree to which a recreation opportunity meets needs.
4. From a broad management perspective, quality is defined as provision of diverse recreation opportunities.
5. The Recreation Opportunity Spectrum (ROS) is a conceptual framework designed to promote diversity in outdoor recreation opportunities. ROS is based on the following propositions:

   A. Recreation experiences are influenced by the settings in which recreation activities occur.

   B. Recreation settings are defined by environmental, social, and managerial conditions.

   C. Environmental, social, and managerial conditions should vary to create a diversity of recreation opportunities.

6. The diversity inherent in ROS should be extended to more explicitly include a wider variety of recreation opportunities based on alternative combinations of environmental, social, and managerial conditions.
7. More research is needed to determine the ways in which recreation experiences are linked to settings.

Chapter Eight
Managing Outdoor Recreation:
Practices and Planning

Management Practices

The preceding chapters have explored selected aspects of outdoor recreation. The underlying purpose of the studies reviewed has been to gain a better understanding of outdoor recreation with the ultimate goal of enhancing the satisfaction of visitors to outdoor recreation areas. The final group of studies which will be examined in this chapter has focused on more directly applied aspects of managing outdoor recreation. These studies have outlined a series of alternative management practices and have begun to evaluate their effectiveness. Several have also suggested a variety of processes through which outdoor recreation management might be most appropriately planned.

Many writers have suggested a variety of management practices which might be applied to outdoor recreation problems such as crowding, conflicting uses, depreciative behavior, and environmental impacts. These management practices have been organized into classification systems to illustrate the wide spectrum of management alternatives.

One system classifies alternatives on the basis of management strategies (Manning 1979). Management strategies are basic conceptual approaches to management and relate to achievement of a desirable objective. Four basic strategies may be recognized for managing outdoor recreation (Figure 8-1). Two strategies deal with supply and demand: the supply of recreation areas may be increased to accommodate more use or the demand for recreation may be limited through restriction. The other two basic strategies treat supply and demand as fixed and focus on modifying either the character of recreation to reduce its adverse impacts or the resource base to increase its durability.

Within each of these basic strategies, there are a number of sub-strategies. The supply of outdoor recreation areas, for example, may be increased in terms of both space and time. With respect to space, new areas may be added or existing areas might be used more effectively through additional access or facilities. With respect to time, some recreational use might be shifted to off-peak periods.

Within the strategy of limiting use, restrictions might be placed on the amount of use accommodated through restricting the number of visitors or their length of stay. Alternatively, certain types of use might be restricted which can be demonstrated to have high social or environmental impacts.

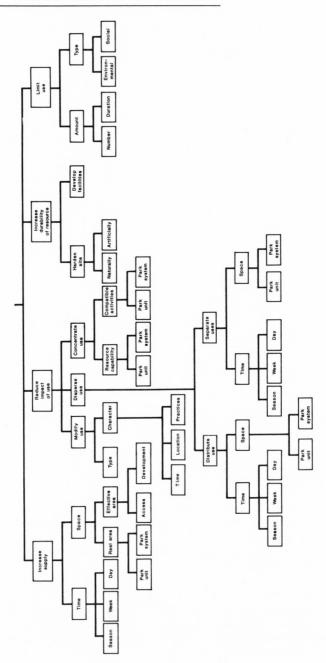

Figure 8-1. Strategies for managing outdoor recreation. (From Manning 1979)

The third basic strategy suggests limiting the social or environmental impacts of existing use. This might be accomplished by modifying the type or character of use, or by dispersing or concentrating use according to user compatibility or resource capability.

Finally, impacts of recreation use might also be limited by increasing the durability of the resource. This might be accomplished by hardening the resource itself (through intensive maintenance, for example) or development of facilities to accommodate use more directly.

A second system of classifying management practices focuses on tactics. Management tactics are direct actions or tools applied by managers to accomplish management strategy. Restrictions on length of stay, differential fees, and use permits, for example, are tactics designed to accomplish the strategy of limiting recreation use. Tactics are often classified according to the directness with which they act on visitor behavior (Peterson and Lime 1979). Direct management practices act directly on visitor behavior, leaving little or no freedom of choice. Indirect management practices attempt to influence the decision factors which lead to visitor behavior (Figure 8-2). For example, a

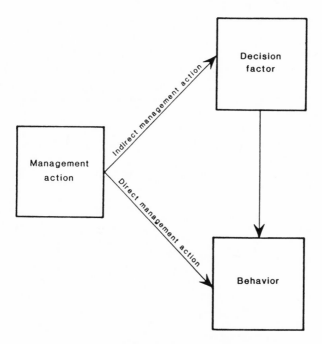

Figure 8-2. Diagram of direct versus indirect management tactics. (Adapted from Peterson and Lime 1979)

direct management approach aimed at reducing campfires in a wilderness environment would be a regulation barring campfires and enforcement of this regulation, while an indirect approach might be an education program designed to inform visitors of the undesirable ecological and aesthetic impacts of campfires and to encourage them to carry and use portable stoves instead. A series of direct and indirect management tactics is shown in Table 8-1.

Table 8-1.   Direct and indirect management tactics.

Type	Example
Direct (Emphasis on regulation of behavior; individual choice restricted; high degree of control)	Impose fines Increase surveillance of area Zone incompatible uses spatially (hiker only zones, prohibit motor use, etc.) Zone uses over time Limit camping in some campsites to one night, or some other limit Rotate use (open or close roads, access points, trails, campsites, etc.) Require reservations Assign campsites and/or travel routes to each camper group in backcountry Limit usage via access point Limit size of groups, number of horses, vehicles, etc. Limit camping to designated campsites only Limit length of stay in area (max./min.) Restrict building campfires Restrict fishing or hunting
Indirect (Emphasis on influencing or modifying behavior, individual retains freedom to choose; control less complete, more variation in use possible)	Improve (or not) access roads, trails Improve (or not) campsites and other concentrated use areas Improve (or not) fish or wildlife populations (stock, allow to die out, etc.) Advertise specific attributes of the area Identify the range of recreation opportunities in surrounding area Educate users to basic concepts of ecology Advertise underused areas and general patterns of use Charge constant entrance fee Charge differential fees by trail, zone, season, etc. Require proof of ecological knowledge and recreational activity skills

Adapted from Lime (1977c; 1979)

Traditionally, it has been suggested that direct regulation of visitors be minimized to the extent possible (Lucas 1982a). This principle of minimum regulation was originally applied to wilderness management (Hendee et al. 1977b), but has been generally extended to all recreation environments. Lucas, for example, has suggested that:

> Recreation and visitor regulations are inherently contradictory. Recreation is a voluntary, pleasurable, rewarding activity, based on free choice, while regulations are designed to restrict free choice (Lucas 1982b, p. 148).

Emphasis on indirect management practices, however, has not been uniformly endorsed (McAvoy and Dustin 1983). It has been argued that indirect practices may be ineffective; there will always be some visitors, for example, who will ignore management efforts to influence the decision factors which lead to behavior. The action of a few may, therefore, hamper attainment of certain management objectives. It has been argued, in fact, that a direct, regulatory approach to management can ultimately lead to more freedom rather than less (Dustin and McAvoy 1984). When all visitors are required to conform to mutually agreed upon behavior, management objectives are more likely to be attained and a diversity of opportunities preserved.

Perhaps the most reasonable conclusion to evolve from this discussion is that when indirect management practices can be shown to be effective, they should be favored. However, when management objectives can only be attained through direct management practices, this approach should be adopted.

Classification of management practices might be based on many factors or concepts. The two approaches described above simply illustrate the array of alternatives available for outdoor recreation management. For any given problem, there are likely several potential solutions. Explicit consideration should be given to this variety of approaches rather than reliance on those which are familiar or simply administratively expedient.

Evaluating Management Practices

An emerging body of research has focused on the effectiveness of selected management practices, particularly indirect approaches. Many of these studies have tested the effectiveness of information and education programs in redistributing the typically uneven spatial and temporal patterns of recreation use described in Chapter Two[1] (Brown and Hunt 1969; Lime and Lucas 1977;

---

[1] A number of studies have documented, using computer-based travel models, the effectiveness of spatial and temporal use redistribution in reducing interparty contacts (Gilbert et al. 1972; Romesburg 1974; Smith and Krutilla 1974; Smith and Headly 1975; Smith and Krutilla 1976; McCool et al. 1977; Peterson et al. 1977; Shechter and Lucas 1978; deBettencourt et al. 1978; Peterson and deBettencourt 1979; Peterson and Lime 1980; Manning and Potter 1984; Potter and Manning 1984). It has been shown, for example, that a nearly 20 percent cut in total use would be required to achieve the same reduction in interparty contacts obtainable through use redistributions (Potter and Manning 1984).

Echelberger et al. 1978; Ormrod and Trahan 1977; Lucas 1981; Roggenbuck and Berrier 1981; Krumpe and Brown 1982; Roggenbuck and Berrier 1982; Echelberger et al. 1983b). These studies have illustrated nearly uniformly that these programs can influence visitor behavior.

Lime and Lucas (1977), for example, studied the effectiveness of providing visitors with information on current use patterns as a way to alter future use patterns. Visitors who had permits for the most heavily used entry points in the Boundary Waters Canoe Area, Minnesota, during 1974 were mailed an information packet including a description of use patterns, noting in particular heavily used areas and times. A survey of a sample of this group who again visited the study area the following year showed that three-fourths of the respondents felt this information was useful, and about one-third were influenced in their choice of entry point, route, or time of subsequent visits. A study in the Shining Rock Wilderness Area, North Carolina (Roggenbuck and Berrier 1981, 1982) experimented with two types of information programs designed to disperse camping away from a heavily used meadow. Two treatment groups were created. A brochure explaining resource impacts associated with concentrated camping and showing the location of other nearby camping areas was given to one treatment group while the other was given the brochure in addition to personal contact with a wilderness ranger. Both groups dispersed their camping activity to a greater degree than a control group, but there was no statistically significant difference between the two treatment groups.

A similar experiment was conducted on trail use in the backcountry of Yellowstone National Park (Krumpe and Brown 1982). A sample group of hikers was given a guidebook which described the attributes of lesser-used trails prior to obtaining a backcountry permit. Through a later survey and examination of permits it was found that 37 percent of this group had selected one of the lesser-used trails compared to 14 percent of a control group. Results also indicated that the earlier the information was received the more influence it had on behavior.

Related studies have also indicated that visitor behavior can be affected by additional information. Simple knowledge of alternative recreation places, for example, has a substantial effect on recreation use patterns: park visitors in one Michigan county were found to be relatively poorly informed about local park opportunities and this affected their choices (Stynes 1982). Moreover, a study of visitors to the Three Sisters Wilderness Area, Oregon, found that visitor knowledge of low-impact camping techniques had a strong effect on behavior: knowledge level explained 35 percent of the variance in low-impact camping practices (Robertson 1982).

Unfortunately, other research indicates that current information and education programs are not very effective in communicating with visitors. Ross and Moeller (1974) tested visitor knowledge of rules and regulations at two campgrounds on the Allegheny National Forest, Pennsylvania, using a ten-item true or false examination. Only 48 percent of the respondents answered six or more of the questions correctly. A similar study of visitors to the Selway-Bitterroot Wilderness Area, Idaho, tested knowledge about wilderness use and management (Fazio 1979a). Only about half of the twenty questions were answered correctly by the average respondent. However, there were significant differences among types of respondents, type of knowledge, and the accuracy of various sources of information, providing indications of where and how information and education programs might be channeled most effectively. Finally, Fazio (1979b) analyzed wilderness management literature mailed in response to visitor requests. Only a portion of the literature was appropriately related to the request, and that portion was judged only moderately effective in aiding management.

Another indirect management practice which has demonstrated considerable potential involves incentives or simple appeals to visitors to reduce depreciative behavior (e.g., litter, vandalism) or its effects (Burgess et al. 1971; Clark et al. 1971b; Clark et al. 1972a; Clark et al. 1972b; Muth and Clark 1978; Christensen 1981; Christensen and Clark 1983). Appeals to visitors by rangers and others was found to significantly reduce litter and littering behavior through direct intervention by visitors with persons observed littering, reporting of littering to managers, and direct removal of litter.

Another group of studies has evaluated more direct management practices, particularly rationing or use limitation techniques. Several studies are theoretical, examining the potential advantages and disadvantages of alternative techniques such as reservation systems, lotteries, pricing, merit, and first-come, first-served systems (Hardin 1969; Hendee and Lucas 1973; Behan 1974; Hendee and Lucas 1974; Stankey and Baden 1977; Fractor 1982).

Other studies are empirical, testing the effectiveness of these use limitation techniques. For example, several rationing systems require visitors to obtain permits to gain entry to recreation areas. Compliance rates have been found to be relatively high, ranging from 68 to 97 percent: most areas are in the 90 percent range (Lime and Lorence 1974; Godin and Leonard 1977a; VanWagtendonk and Benedict 1980; Plager and Womble 1981; Parsons et al. 1982). Mandatory permit requirements have been evaluated highly by visitors, even by those who were unable to obtain a permit (Fazio and Gilbert 1974; Stankey 1979). Moreover, permit systems that have incorporated trailhead quotas have been found effective in redistributing use both spatially and temporally (Hulbert and Higgans 1977; VanWagtendonk 1981).

A common precursor to mandatory permit systems is voluntary self-registration. Visitors are asked to register themselves at trailheads as a measure of use for management purposes. Compliance with this management practice has been found to be considerably less uniform than with mandatory permits: registration rates have been found to vary from 21 to 89 percent, with most in the 65 to 80 percent range (Wenger 1964; Wenger and Gregerson 1964; James and Schreuder 1971; Lucas et al. 1971; James and Schreuder 1972; Lucas 1975;

Scotter 1981; Leatherberry and Lime 1981; Lucas and Kovalicky 1981). Several types of visitors have especially low registration rates, including day users, hunters, horseback riders, and single person parties.

Recreation fees have been subject to limited testing as a management tool. It has been suggested that differential fees—higher prices for peak periods and locations—might redistribute recreation use patterns more evenly over both space and time (Manning et al. 1982; Manning and Powers 1984). Research findings have been mixed. LaPage et al. (1975) found that creation of a $1.00 differential between waterfront and non-waterfront campsites at a New Hampshire state park did not affect campsite occupancy rates. Similar studies in Massachusetts and Vermont state parks, however, found statistically significant changes in occupancy rates after implementation of differential fees, although shifts in use were not large (Willis et al. 1975; Manning et al. 1984). All three of these experimental studies used relatively small fee differentials, ranging from 50¢ to $2.00, indicating that larger differentials will likely be needed to effect more substantive changes.

Management Planning

It is evident that outdoor recreation managers must ultimately make value judgments about the types of opportunities to be provided. This is an inevitable consequence of the diversity of public tastes for outdoor recreation and the variety of management practices available. The role of value judgments in determining management objectives was highlighted in the consideration of carrying capacity in Chapter Four.

But value judgments should not be arbitrary or implied. They should be an explicit and visible part of a systematic and well-documented planning process. In this way management judgments might be developed in a more orderly and rational way, subject to public and professional participation and review.

A number of writers have addressed this need for a systematic management planning process (Gold 1973; Brown 1977; Brown et al. 1979; Frissell et al. 1980; Chilman et al. 1981; Hunt and Brooks 1983; Stankey et al. 1984; Stankey et al. 1985). Though there is considerable variety in the processes suggested, each is based on the inherent logic of planning itself, which involves four basic steps: (1) determine the current situation; (2) decide what situation is desired; (3) establish how to get from the current to the desired situation; and (4) monitor and evaluate progress or success in attaining the desired situation.

These four fundamental steps can and should be translated rather directly into an outdoor recreation planning process comprised of four corresponding steps, each of which typically involves a number of substeps. A management planning process based on these steps is described in Chapter Nine.

Summary and Conclusions

1. *A variety of strategies and tactics is available for managing outdoor recreation.*

2. *Explicit consideration should be given to all potential management practices rather than relying on those which are familiar or expedient.*

3. *Indirect management practices should be favored over direct practices where they can be shown to be effective. However, direct management practices are justified where they are needed to attain management objectives.*

4. *A variety of both indirect and direct management practices has been demonstrated to be effective in influencing recreation use patterns. In particular, information and education programs, mandatory permit systems, and differential fees have been shown to be effective management practices.*

5. *Outdoor recreation management planning should be conducted through a systematic, well-documented process which is subject to public participation and review. In this way, necessary value judgments should be explicit, rational, and defensible.*

Chapter Nine
Managing Outdoor Recreation: Knowledge into Action

Synthesis

At the beginning of this book it was suggested that management implications of outdoor recreation research become evident after the findings from a number of studies have been reviewed and synthesized. The purpose of this final chapter, then, is to synthesize the body of knowledge presented in the book on a broader scale to develop a series of management implications. This task is approached in two stages. First, ten basic principles of outdoor recreation are suggested. These principles are necessarily broad and are drawn from findings and notions which recurred throughout the preceding chapters. Second, a planning process is developed to guide management of outdoor recreation, incorporating these principles of outdoor recreation. Finally, several observations are offered on outdoor recreation research and its relationship to management.

Principles of Outdoor Recreation

Principle 1. Outdoor recreation management should be considered within a three-fold framework of concerns: the natural environment, the social environment, and the management environment. The multidisciplinary nature of outdoor recreation noted at the beginning of the book became more evident as a wide variety of research approaches was described. The basic three-fold approach to outdoor recreation was developed in the analysis of outdoor recreation carrying capacity and was also found useful in the description of outdoor recreation opportunities. Each component holds potentially important implications for defining outdoor recreation and failure to consider each component will leave outdoor recreation unmanaged in important and potentially costly ways. This three-fold organizational framework is a useful way to consider and analyze outdoor recreation issues in a comprehensive, multidisciplinary fashion.

Principle 2. There is great diversity in public tastes for outdoor recreation. This is true in regard to, among other things, activities engaged in, attitudes and preferences about management policy, desired use density or contact levels, and motivations for outdoor recreation. This diversity in tastes stems, at least in part, from varying socio-economic characteristics and cultural influences. Simple averages or majority opinions often used to report or summarize outdoor recreation research tend to obscure this diversity.

Principle 3. Diversity is needed in outdoor recreation opportunities. Recognition of diversity in tastes for outdoor recreation as suggested in Principle 2 leads logically to the notion that diversity is also needed in outdoor recreation opportunities. The natural, social, and management environments that define outdoor recreation opportunities should be combined in a variety of alternative arrangements to produce diversity in the total outdoor recreation system. In this way, a greater variety of visitors' preferences can be met and satisfaction maximized.

Principle 4. Explicit objectives are needed to guide management of outdoor recreation. If outdoor recreation opportunities are to be provided to meet a variety of tastes, they must be designed and managed explicitly for these purposes. Objectives help guide management decisions which otherwise might be unduly influenced by majority opinions, an outspoken minority, or those insensitive to management factors such as use density, resource quality, or controversial management practices. While management objectives are ultimately based on value judgments, they should be formulated on the basis of resource, social, and management factors.

Principle 5. Satisfaction of visitors to outdoor recreation areas is a multifaceted concept. Visitors are perceptive of and sensitive to many aspects of the natural, social, and management environments that comprise outdoor recreation areas. Though some aspects are more important than others, many considerations are likely to affect visitor satisfaction. Management of outdoor recreation should be broad-based, providing explicit attention to as many of these aspects as are known and manageable.

Principle 6. Outdoor recreation is more appropriately defined in terms of fulfilling motivations than participation in activities. Though participation in activities is the outward manifestation of outdoor recreation, it is motivations for selected values, rewards, or satisfactions that ultimately drive participation. Consideration of motivations in outdoor recreation management will lead to a more fundamental understanding of visitors and their satisfaction.

Principle 7. Quality in outdoor recreation is the degree to which opportunities satisfy the motivations for which they are designed. Principles 2 and 3 addressed the diversity of tastes in outdoor recreation and the need for corresponding diversity in opportunities. This principle suggests that correspondence between tastes and opportunities is the most appropriate criterion for determining quality in outdoor recreation. Implicit in this principle is the notion that type and quality of outdoor recreation are distinct concepts. Many types of outdoor recreation opportunities exist and each can and should be of high quality. High quality exists when outdoor recreation opportunities meet the needs of visitors.

Principle 8. Differences in the perceptions of outdoor recreation visitors and managers require a concerted effort to obtain systematic and objective information about and from visitors. Research indicates that managers' perceptions of the visitors to outdoor recreation areas often differ from reality. If a basic purpose of managing outdoor recreation is to provide satisfaction to visitors, then objective and systematically collected information is needed about what affects satisfaction.

Principle 9. Outdoor recreation opportunities should be managed for relatively homogeneous groups of visitors. Research suggests that motivations for recreation and attitudes, preferences, and perceptions of the total recreation environment are related within groups of visitors. To the extent possible, combinations of environmental, social, and managerial conditions should be designed to be compatible in view of these relationships. In this way, recreation opportunities will be managed for selected market segments of the visitor population. This will help ensure that visitors attracted to the same areas share similar values, and perceptions of alikeness among visitors will tend to be enhanced, thus potentially increasing the social capacity of these areas.

Principle 10. A variety of practices is available for managing outdoor recreation. Explicit consideration should be given to all potential management practices rather than relying on those which are familiar or expedient. In general, indirect management practices should be favored over direct practices where they can be shown to be effective. Management practices should be determined through a systematic, well-documented process which is subject to public participation and review.

A Management Planning Process

This section outlines a process by which management policy for outdoor recreation areas might be formulated. It should be emphasized that what is suggested is a process, not a prescription. As the principles of the previous section suggest, tastes in outdoor recreation, and the opportunities needed to satisfy them, are too diverse for standard management approaches to be appropriate. Instead, as described in Chapter Eight, what is needed is a logical and comprehensive process by which rational and defensible management approaches can be formulated.

The process outlined in this section borrows and builds upon the planning processes noted in Chapter Eight. In particular, it relies on the Limits of Acceptable Change model outlined by Stankey and associates (Stankey and McCool 1984; Stankey et al. 1984; Stankey et al. 1985). In addition, it

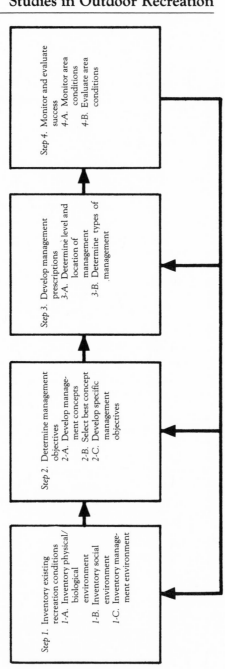

Figure 9-1.   A management planning process.

incorporates the principles described in the preceding section. The management planning process is described below and illustrated in Figure 9-1.

Step 1. Inventory existing recreation conditions. Management planning for outdoor recreation begins with an inventory and assessment of recreation conditions. The three-fold framework of outdoor recreation suggested in Principle 1 should guide this inventory and assessment process. Baseline data should be gathered for each of the three major components of outdoor recreation: the natural, social, and management environments.

Substep 1-A. Inventory and assess the physical/biological environment of the area. The natural resources of an outdoor recreation area are often a principal focus of visitors and outdoor recreation agencies are often charged with maintaining some degree of protection for natural resource values. Information on the extent, location, and quality of the natural resource base is therefore important in formulating management policy. Pertinent questions to be answered in the natural resources inventory and assessment process include:

1. Does the area contain unique or outstanding ecological, scientific, educational, historic, or cultural resources that warrant special management attention?
2. Does the area contain critical habitat for threatened or endangered species?
3. How fragile are the area's resources? What are the changes likely to occur as a result of recreational use?
4. In what condition—how natural—are the area's resources currently?

Substep 1-B. Inventory and assess the social environment of the area. This involves a determination of what types of experiences are desired by the public from the area. As suggested in Principle 6, it would be most appropriate to conduct this assessment in terms of visitor motivations. However, since research methods for this type of assessment are complex and still evolving, surrogates for motivations may have to be used, such as visitors' attitudes and preferences, desired activities, and personal characteristics. Recognizing the differences between visitors and non-visitors to outdoor recreation areas, some effort should be made to include interested non-visitors in this process. Behavioral or observational measures of actual visitor use patterns should supplement the survey approach when and where possible. The major emphasis of this effort, as suggested in Principle 8, is to obtain systematic and objective information from and about visitors. Pertinent questions to be answered in the social inventory and assessment process include:

1. What kinds of recreation does the area now support?
2. What are the recreation motivations of people attracted to the area?
3. What are the attitudes and preferences toward management policies, facilities, and services?
4. What are the socio-economic and cultural characteristics of people attracted to the area?

Substep 1-C. Inventory and assess the management environment of the area. The way in which an outdoor recreation area is managed affects both the condition of the natural resource base and the types of recreation experiences provided. In addition, management is often constrained by various institutional dictates. The management inventory and assessment process should determine both potentials and constraints. Pertinent questions to be answered in this process include:

1. What management practices are currently applied to the area?
2. What legislative and policy dictates apply to the area?
3. What personnel and financial resources are available for area management?

The comprehensive description of current recreation conditions collected in Step 1 will provide input for Step 2 of the management planning process.

Step 2. Determine management objectives. The process of formulating explicit management objectives as suggested in Principle 4 begins with broad management concepts and works toward specific, quantifiable objectives. It starts with the baseline data collected in Step 1 and incorporates public involvement and considered value judgments.

Substep 2-A. Develop alternative management concepts. The three-fold framework of outdoor recreation suggested in Principle 1 is again instructive in this context. Theoretically, the three factors involved in outdoor recreation—the natural environment, social or experiential conditions, and the type of management applied—can be combined in widely ranging configurations. But broad management directions need to be established for each of the three basic factors.

Initial assessment of the inventory data gathered in Step 1 will normally suggest general management directions. Legislative or agency policy directives, for example, will often describe, at least in a general fashion, the type of recreation experiences to be provided and the emphasis to be placed on maintaining natural resource conditions. The Wilderness Act, for instance, states that areas included in the National Wilderness Preservation System should be managed to emphasize solitude and naturalness. The financial and budgetary resources available for management can also influence management direction; high use levels are generally not feasible without concomitant budgets and personnel to accommodate them. Natural resource factors can also pose important constraints on general management direction. Unique or fragile resources, for example, suggest relatively low use levels and low-impact activities. Finally, the outdoor recreation experiences desired by the public influence management directions. Public preferences should be accommodated to the extent possible, given the constraints of natural resource and management conditions.

Normally, there will be several, perhaps many, management concepts feasible for an area. This is a reflection of the diversity of natural resource, social, and management conditions found and the variety of configurations in which they may be arranged. The situation is made even more complex in large areas which might appropriately be divided into two or more use areas or zones, each reflecting a different combination of conditions. But to encourage realistic and efficient public input and evaluation management concepts must be limited to those few which reflect, in the initial judgment of planners and managers, the most realistic and reasonable alternatives.

Development of alternative management concepts is not a simple task, though several circumstances may reduce its complexity. First, the constraints imposed by natural resource, social, or management factors may limit realistic management alternatives. Second, some measure of public opinion should already have been gained through the social inventory process (Step 1-B) to suggest what types of management alternatives might ultimately be found acceptable by the public. Third, planning in general, particularly in the public sector, tends to be incremental in nature, seldom making changes which differ drastically from current conditions. Thus, realistic management alternatives will often reflect, at least to some degree, current conditions (Brown 1977). Fourth, as suggested in Principles 2 and 3, tastes in outdoor recreation are diverse and opportunities for outdoor recreation should also be diverse. Part of the process of designing for diversity should involve comparison of the area under consideration with similar areas on a regional or national basis. It may then be appropriate to focus on opportunities which are currently in short supply and for which there appears to be additional demand. The desirability of diversity also suggests that, if the area is extensive enough, management concepts might provide a range of uses, particularly if the area is unique or outstanding in some way. Fifth, Principle 9 suggests that outdoor recreation opportunities be designed and managed for relatively homogeneous groups. Thus the management concepts developed should reflect combinations of environmental, social, and managerial conditions that are compatible in the minds of the public.

Though these guidelines may help the development of management concepts, the process still depends on the considered judgment of outdoor recreation planners and managers. It should be remembered from Principle 4 that the process of developing management objectives, though it should be based on objective data, ultimately involves value judgments.

Substep 2-B. Select the best management concept. This involves systematic evaluation of the alternative concepts developed in the previous step. This evaluation can be facilitated by systematically examining and describing the effects of each concept. Pertinent considerations include 1) the contribution of each concept to diversity in the total outdoor recreation system, 2) the potential effects of each concept on visitor use of the area, 3) the natural resource and social values that are enhanced or diminished by each concept, and 4) the management feasibility of accomplishing each concept.

There are no precise methods for weighing these effects and determining the best management concept. A considerable amount of management judgment is again involved. But a program of public involvement is also essential. Interested members of the public should be informed of the management concepts under consideration and have the opportunity to comment on them. This process of public input may produce new concepts for consideration or, more likely, combinations or modifications of the original concepts. There may also be little or no consensus among the public. However, after an appropriate period of public involvement, a decision must be made by managers to provide broad management direction for the area.

Substep 2-C. Develop specific management objectives.[1] The general prescriptions of Step 2-B need to be made more specific so they can guide day-to-day management and be used eventually to evaluate management success. These specific descriptors are called management objectives and should be expressed in as explicit and quantifiable terms as possible.

As in the preceding two steps, a considerable amount of judgment is needed in translating management concepts into management objectives. Several factors can help guide this process. First, the management concepts themselves indicate which factors in the total recreation environment are to be emphasized and suggest a general range of conditions for these factors. A management concept emphasizing solitude as an important factor of the social environment of the area, for example, would logically lead to an emphasis on managing contacts between parties and would suggest that contacts be kept to a relatively small number. Hence the decision to set an actual number of contacts as the management objective is to be made within somewhat limited parameters. Studies of wilderness recreation report that trail encounters in the range of two to four per day are preferred by many visitors. The decision, however, between two, three, or four trail encounters per day as the management objective in a wilderness area is not a matter of precise determination. Rather it is a judgment which should be based on a variety of factors, many of them site specific, such as demand for use of the area (high demand might suggest four trail encounters per day to accommodate more visitors) and the diversity of types of use (different types of users might suggest two trail encounters per day due to lower tolerances for encounters with other types of users).

---

[1] As indicated throughout this discussion, management objectives should be developed for important elements of the natural, social, and management environments. However, in keeping with the social science emphasis of this book, management objectives are here considered primarily in terms of visitor perceptions and discussion is limited to those elements of these environments that research indicates visitors are aware of and which potentially affect satisfaction. There will likely be other elements, particularly of the natural and management environments, of which visitors are unaware, but which still require explicit management attention and objectives.

Table 9-1. Potentially important elements of the outdoor recreation environment.

Natural environment	Social environment	Management environment
Trail erosion	Number of trail encounters	Use limitations
Campsite erosion	Number of camp encoun-	Type of use limitation
Campsite groundcover	ters	Control over route or itin-
Damage to trees/shrubs	Type of groups encountered	erary
Water quality	Size of groups encountered	Use fee
Presence of wildlife	Behavior of groups en-	Zoning
Litter	countered	Type of access
Vandalism	Location of encounters be-	Party size limits
Shading of campsites	tween groups	Trail standards
Location proximate to	Perceptions of alikeness be-	Campsite standards
water body or other at-	tween parties	Law enforcement
traction	Noise	Rules and regulations
Opportunities for activities	Rule violations	Information/education
(e.g. fishing, hunting)	Perceptions of naturalness	programs
	of the environment	Presence of rangers
	Perceptions of regimenta-	Presence of sanitary facil-
	tion by management	ities
	Perceptions of opportuni-	Type of sanitary facilities
	ties to fulfill selected mo-	
	tivations (e.g. closeness to	
	nature, risk, avoid	
	crowds)	

Second, research can indicate which factors of the total recreation environment should be the subject of management objectives. As noted in Principle 5, satisfaction of visitors is a multifaceted concept; thus, there will often be a relatively large number of factors for which management objectives should be developed. Public input and the research-based literature reviewed in the first eight chapters of this book both provide an indication of management factors important to a variety of recreation visitors. Selected factors are listed in Table 9-1.

Third, management objectives should reflect a range of conditions for factors important to visitors to incorporate a desirable element of diversity. Thus each area is considered as an integrated component of the total outdoor recreation system rather than as a separate and isolated entity.

At the conclusion of Step 2, specific and quantifiable management objectives should have been established for each factor of concern.

Step 3. Develop management prescriptions. The process now turns to determining how to get from the current to the desired situation. This involves deciding what level and type of management actions are to be applied to the area.

Substep 3-A. Determine the level and location of management needed. This will be determined by the congruence between current conditions as determined in the inventory and desired conditions as specified by management objectives. Obviously, the wider the difference between existing and desired conditions, the greater will be the management efforts needed to meet objectives.

Substep 3-B. Determine the type of management needed. These decisions can be complex and value-laden but, again, several factors can provide guidance in this process. First, as suggested in Principle 10, a variety of practices is available for managing outdoor recreation. Examining the range of management alternatives can be helpful in developing an appropriate management program.

Second, as also suggested in Principle 10, indirect management practices should generally be favored over direct practices where they can be shown to be effective. The evaluation research described in Chapter Eight indicates several types of management practices shown to be effective.

Third, the management concepts and objectives developed in Step 2 define the recreation environment that is to be created and maintained. Management practices should be selected to be as compatible as possible with this environment.

Step 4. Monitor and evaluate success. This is a critical but sometimes neglected step in any planning and management process. Once a management program has been developed and implemented it is necessary to periodically assess whether desired conditions are being achieved and maintained. In outdoor recreation management this involves measuring the degree to which management objectives have been attained and evaluating future management needs.

Substep 4-A. Monitor area conditions. This involves periodic measurement of area conditions, focusing on those conditions identified in management objectives. An effective monitoring program will be greatly facilitated if management objectives are specific and quantifiable as suggested above.

An important issue to be addressed in designing the monitoring program concerns how frequently variables should be measured. There are no precise guidelines for making this determination, as site conditions and budgetary circumstances will often be pivotal considerations. However, Stankey et al. (1985) list several circumstances which would normally dictate more frequent monitoring than normal: 1) when area conditions are close to those specified by management objectives, 2) when rates of environmental, social, or managerial change are thought to be high, 3) when the initial inventory and data base for the area are incomplete or of inadequate quality, 4) when the potential effectiveness of management actions is not well known or predictable, and 5) where there have been unanticipated changes to the area such as additional access or changes in adjacent land uses.

Substep 4-B. Evaluate area conditions. Evaluation involves comparing area conditions to those specified in management objectives and determining whether success has been attained or if any changes are needed. As noted in Principle 7, quality in outdoor recreation is generally defined as the degree to which opportunities satisfy the motivations for which they are designed so that theoretically, this would involve measuring the satisfaction level of visitors with selected motivations. Realistically, however, evaluation will usually be focused on management objectives. This is a reasonable alternative as management objectives were determined on the basis of the motivations, attitudes, and preferences of selected visitor groups, so that attainment of the conditions specified in management objectives should result in visitor satisfaction.

A final evaluation issue involves the cyclic aspects of the management planning process. Under routine circumstances, evaluation focuses on Step 3, analyzing what if any changes in management are needed to achieve management objectives which are, in this context, considered fixed. At some point, however, it will be appropriate to reevaluate management objectives; in this case evaluation focuses on Step 2. Changes in management objectives, of course, should only be made consciously and explicitly, following the procedures outlined in Step 2. Evaluations of this scope will normally need to be done only infrequently, perhaps every ten years or so. Finally, there will come a time when baseline data for the area is outdated or no longer adequate, and then evaluation must focus on Step 1. An evaluation of this scope, however, will likely be very infrequent, perhaps only every twenty years or so.

Observations on the Management Planning Process. Several of the most critical decisions to be made in management planning are difficult and complex value judgments. Though these decisions are guided by research findings, public input, and reason, they still, at times, seem to be almost arbitrary. But it should be remembered that these decisions are nearly always subject to change or revision should the need arise. Indeed, the monitoring and evaluation process builds in such opportunities on a periodic basis. Thus, while these decisions should be approached with all due care and consideration, they are not immutable and should not forestall the management planning process.

The management planning process should be approached and applied aggressively. Much of the emphasis of this book, developed directly out of the research literature, has been on the need for diversity in outdoor recreation. The evidence suggests that if outdoor recreation areas are not planned and managed explicitly for a variety of types of opportunities, they are likely to become increasingly similar with the result that values which are sensitive or nondominant are likely to disappear from the total outdoor recreation system (Dustin and McAvoy 1982; Schreyer and Knopf 1984). Unfortunately, there is evidence to suggest that management planning is not moving ahead aggressively, and that the predominate management approach is reactive. A recent survey of managers of wilderness and related areas found that nearly half of all areas had yet to begin to come to grips with the general issue of carrying capacity (Washburne and Cole 1983). Creativity in management is a closely related issue. Lucas (1973) has observed that the current emphasis of recreation management seems to be placed at the extremes of the opportunity spectrum—wilderness and developed areas. More emphasis on creative opportunities between these extremes is needed to more fully accomplish the objective of diversity.

Management planning is an iterative process involving feedback loops. The first two steps of the process, for example—inventory of existing conditions and formulation of management objectives—are not necessarily discrete activities which can be conducted in isolation from one another. It is difficult to determine what specific factors to inventory from existing conditions without some notion of what management objectives might be. Conversely, it may be unrealistic to set management objectives without some notion of the existing recreation environment. In reality, management planning may involve several cycles through the process.

Management of the social environment in outdoor recreation should emphasize more than interparty contacts. Concern over crowding has captured the attention of managers and researchers for many years; the number of studies reviewed in Chapter Five is ample evidence of this emphasis. But this research has shown that crowding is a complex phenomenon and that factors other than interparty contacts are important to visitors and affect their satisfaction. Interparty contacts will often be an important management variable, but they do not, in and of themselves, define the social environment of outdoor recreation.

Good information is needed for the management planning process. Decisions will only be rational and creditable if they are based on adequate, objective information. This need is made more pressing by the inherent diversity in outdoor recreation. The diversity among visitors has already been addressed, but there is diversity as well in natural environments and management systems. Certainly outdoor recreation areas vary dramatically in their uniqueness, resiliency, and location. Moreover, Chapter 8 illustrated the variety of management practices available, and several studies have documented their widespread application by outdoor recreation agencies (Schoenfeld 1976; Bury and Fish 1980; Fish and Bury 1981; Washburne and Cole 1983). Good information with regard to all of these matters, much of it site-specific, will be needed to make the management planning process work.

Information is also needed from management. Quality in outdoor recreation is defined as the degree to which opportunities satisfy the motivations for which they are designed, but unless managers can help guide visitors to the types of opportunities they seek, motivations are not likely to be well-satisfied.

Finally, it seems appropriate to return to the issue of value judgments and the necessary burden they place on managers. In the early years of outdoor recreation research, Wagar (1964), in his original monograph on carrying capacity, concluded that, "As much as public officials might wish to shift the burden to impersonal equations, the formulas devised by researchers can guide but not supplant human judgment." Since then researchers have devised and developed numerous equations, formulas, relationships, concepts, hypotheses, and theories that can be incorporated into management planning—but, as ironic as it may seem, the burden of value judgments remains inescapable.

Relating Research and Management

It was noted at the beginning of this book that outdoor recreation research is frequently criticized because it has few practical implications. One of the purposes of the study reported in this book was to illustrate that research, when viewed collectively and comprehensively, has a number of important implications for outdoor recreation management.

But criticism of outdoor recreation research and the equally disparaging views of management expressed occasionally by researchers stem from a number of misunderstandings and misconceptions about the research and management processes and the relationships between them. Part of the problem arises from the distinctions between basic and applied research (Johnson and Field 1981; Field and Johnson 1983). Traditionally, research within the academic environment has tended to be more basic than applied. It is oriented toward enhancing knowledge or testing theory within a conventional academic discipline, and hence has a closely defined social context; a relatively small group of peers, narrowly defined limits on subject matter, and a reward system driven largely by scholarly publications. Managers often view this traditional model of research with frustration and impatience; they complain that research problems are defined too narrowly and abstractly to have much application and that research reports are overly technical and obtuse.

Applied research, on the other hand, is oriented toward gaining immediately useful empirical knowledge and often involves interdisciplinary concerns. Research must be done quickly, irrespective of academic schedules, and primary focus must be placed on variables which are manageable and not just those which enhance understanding. But this model of research is often frustrating to academics; the problems are not defined so as to be amenable to research, and frequently involve concerns outside the researcher's discipline, and the academic reward system does not traditionally recognize successful application of research results.

Communication and compromise between researchers and managers is clearly needed to derive a model of research that is both rewarding and useful. Managers and researchers must realize the need for both basic and applied research. The ultimate goal of any research program is to provide useful information. But research results will be most useful when considered within a theoretical framework. Without a theoretical framework, research results remain isolated facts rather than being synthesized into a body of knowledge. In fact, one of the most stinging criticisms of recreation research is that it has lacked an adequate theoretical foundation (Smith 1975; Groves and Wolensky 1977; Driver and Knopf 1981; Tinsley 1984; Burch 1984; Riddick et al. 1984).

Perhaps the most important element of cooperation between managers and researchers concerns communication at the time the research problem is defined (Schweitzer and Randall 1974; Stankey 1980c). Applied research suggests that managers provide the initiative for research so that they can ensure that their problems will be addressed as directly as possible. But researchers also need to be involved in the process of problem definition to ensure that the problems identified by managers are valid research issues. The relationship between recreation use and changes in the recreation environment, for example, has both researchable and non-researchable elements. Researchers can determine the nature of these relationships, but establishing limits of acceptable change involves value judgments which are not subject to solution through research. In short, managers and researchers must work together to define the problem, so that the outcome of research will be fulfilling to both parties.

Communication of research results is also critical. When reporting applied aspects of research, a different audience must be addressed than when writing for scientific journals. Johnson and Field note that:

> . . . academic diction is frequently riddled with jargon, fashionable intellectual clichés, and even occasional foreign phrases. Applied research findings, however, must be communicated in clear, concise, and understandable composition. The intent is not to impress readers with the writer's intellect, but to convey in a straightforward manner the practical significance of the research results for which the client has paid (Johnson and Field 1981, pp. 275-276).

It has been suggested that go-betweens are needed to bridge the communications gap between researchers and managers (McCool and Schreyer 1977). Extension agents fill this role in other fields and may be an appropriate model for outdoor recreation (Groves and Wolensky 1977). Pilot and demonstration projects may also be an effective way to communicate research results (Stankey 1980c). Literature review and synthesis should also be recognized as a potentially valuable form of research. Many studies viewed individually have few management implications beyond the study location, but broader implications become more clear when a number of studies are considered together (e.g., Hendee and Potter 1975; Lime 1976). This would seem an especially efficient and productive type of research for managers to encourage.

The management process is also the source of some misunderstandings and misconceptions which divide managers and researchers. Researchers undertaking applied studies must realize that their findings are but one input into the decision-making process. A host of other considerations, loosely labeled "political factors," legitimately affect the final outcome of a management problem, regardless of how scientifically sound the research. Shelby (1981b) has described what is, perhaps, the classic example in outdoor recreation of melding of research and political factors in management decision-making.

Of course, managers too must realize that research is but one input into the decision-making process. Expectations from research must be realistic; research is not likely to solve problems directly. At best, research can describe the probable consequences of alternative courses of action; it is up to managers to determine which consequences are most desirable.

The timing of research also has implications for its effectiveness (Schreyer 1980). Too often research is not begun until a problem has reached crisis proportions. At this point little time is left to conduct an appropriate study, and results must be considered within an atmosphere of highly polarized feelings. Cooperative, long range research planning can help minimize this problem (Peterson and Lime 1978; Shafer and Lucas 1979).

Unfortunately, evidence indicates that communication between managers and researchers is limited. A recent study of federal and state outdoor recreation managers, for example, found that only 6 percent had regular contact with university researchers and 16 percent had regular contact with government agency scientists (McCool and Schreyer 1977). Applied research problems are not likely to be defined appropriately nor are results likely to be communicated effectively under these circumstances. The same study, however, offers hope that communication and cooperation between managers and researchers can be effective. Contact between managers and researchers was positively and strongly related to managers' judgment of the quality of outdoor recreation research.

The last two decades of social science research in outdoor recreation have enhanced understanding of this social phenomenon and offered a number of implications which might help guide management more effectively. Much remains to be done. The success of future research will be determined, to a large degree, by the extent to which researchers and managers understand each others' roles and processes.

Summary and Conclusions

1. *Ten major principles to guide outdoor recreation management can be abstracted from social science research in outdoor recreation:*

    A. *Outdoor recreation management should be considered within a three-fold framework of concerns: 1) the natural environment, 2) the social environment, and 3) the management environment.*

    B. *There is great diversity in public tastes for outdoor recreation.*

    C. *Diversity is needed in outdoor recreation opportunities.*

    D. *Explicit objectives are needed to guide management of outdoor recreation*

    E. *Satisfaction of visitors to outdoor recreation areas is a multifaceted concept.*

    F. *Outdoor recreation is more appropriately defined in terms of fulfilling motivations than participation in activities.*

    G. *Quality in outdoor recreation is the degree to which opportunities satisfy the motivations for which they are designed.*

    H. *Differences in the perceptions of outdoor recreation visitors and managers require a concerted effort to obtain systematic and objective information about and from visitors.*

    I. *Outdoor recreation opportunities should be managed for relatively homogeneous groups of visitors.*

    J. *A variety of practices is available for managing outdoor recreation.*

2. *The above principles are incorporated in an outdoor recreation management planning process illustrated in Figure 9-1.*

3. *The effectiveness of outdoor recreation research will be enhanced by the extent to which managers and researchers communicate and understand each others' roles and processes.*

References

Absher, J. D., and R. G. Lee. 1981. Density as an incomplete cause of crowding in backcountry settings. *Leisure Sciences* 4(3):231-247.

Adams, J. T. 1930. Diminishing returns in modern life. *Harpers* 160:529-537.

Adams, S. W. 1979. Segmentation of a recreational fishing market: A canonical analysis of fishing attributes and party composition. *Journal of Leisure Research* 11(2):82-91

Adelman, B. J. E, T. A. Heberlein, and T. M. Bonnickson. 1982. Social psychological explanations for the persistence of a conflict between paddling canoeists and motorcraft users in the Boundary Waters Canoe Area. *Leisure Sciences* 5(1):45-61.

Alldredge, R. B. 1973. Some capacity theory for parks and recreation areas. *Trends* 10(Oct.-Dec.):20-29.

Altman, I. 1975. *The Environment and Social Behavior: Privacy, Personal Space, Territory, Crowding.* Monterey, California: Brooks/Cole Publishing Company.

Anderson, D. H. 1980. Long-time Boundary Waters' visitors change use patterns. *Naturalist* 3(4):2-5.

Anderson, D. H. 1983. Displacement: one consequence of not meeting people's needs. Pages 31-37 in: *Research in Forest Productivity, Use, and Pest Control.* (M. M. Harris and A. M. Spearing, eds.). USDA Forest Service General Technical Report NE-90.

Anderson, D. H., and P. J. Brown. 1984. The displacement process in recreation. *Journal of Leisure Research* 16(1):61-73.

Anderson, D. H., E. C. Leatherberry, and D. W. Lime. 1978. *An Annotated Bibliography on River Recreation.* USDA Forest Service General Technical Report NC-41.

Atkinson, J. W., and D. Birch. 1972. *Motivation: The Dynamics of Action.* New York: John Wiley and Sons, Inc.

Baldwin, M. F. 1970. *The Off-Road Vehicle and Environmental Quality.* Washington, D.C.: The Conservation Foundation.

Bates, G. H. 1935. The vegetation of footpaths, sidewalks, cart-tracks, and gateways. *Journal of Ecology* 23:470-487.

Baumgartner, R., and T. A. Heberlein. 1981. Process, goal, and social interaction in recreation: What makes an activity substitutable. *Leisure Sciences* 4(4):443-457.

Beaman, J. 1975. Comments on the paper "The substitutability concept: Implications for recreation research and management," by Hendee and Burdge. *Journal of Leisure Research* 7(2):146-152.

Beaman, J., Y. Kim, and S. Smith. 1979. The effect of recreation supply on participation. *Leisure Sciences* 2(1):71-87.

Beard, J. G., and M. G. Ragheb. 1980. Measuring leisure satisfaction. *Journal of Leisure Research* 12(1):20-33.

Beard, J. G., and M. G. Ragheb. 1983. Measuring leisure motivation. *Journal of Leisure Research* 15(3):219-228.

Beardsley, W. 1967. *Cost Implications of Camper and Campground Characteristics in Central Colorado.* USDA Forest Service Research Note RM-86.

Becker, B. W. 1976. Perceived similarities among recreational activities. *Journal of Leisure Research* 8(2):112-122.

Becker, R. H. 1978. Social carrying capacity and user satisfaction: An experiential function. *Leisure Sciences* 1(3):241-257.

Becker, R. H. 1981. Displacement of recreational users between the lower St. Croix and upper Mississippi rivers. *Journal of Environmental Management* 13(3):259-267.

Becker, R. H., and A. Jubenville. 1982. Forest recreation management. Pages 335-355 in: *Forest Science* (R. Young, ed.). New York: John Wiley and Sons.

Becker, R. H., A. Jubenville, and G. W. Burnett. 1984. Fact and judgment in the search for a social carrying capacity. *Leisure Sciences* 6(4):475-486.

Becker, R. H., B. Niemann, and W. Gates. 1981. Displacement of users within a river system: Social and environmental tradeoffs. Pages 33-38 in: *Some Recent Products of River Recreation Research.* USDA Forest Service General Technical Report NC-63.

Behan, R. W. 1974. Police state wilderness: A comment on mandatory wilderness permits. *Journal of Forestry* 72:98-99.

Berger, B. M. 1962. The sociology of leisure: Some suggestions. *Industrial Relations* 1(Feb.):31-45.

Bevins, M. I., and D. P. Wilcox. 1979. *Evaluation of Nationwide Outdoor Recreation Participation Surveys 1959-1978.* Burlington, Vemont: Vermont Agricultural Experiment Station.

Bishop, D. W. 1970. Stability of the factor structure of leisure behavior: Analysis of four communities. *Journal of Leisure Research* 2(3):160-170.

Bishop, D. W., and M. Ikeda. 1970. Status and role factors in the leisure behavior of different occupations. *Sociology and Social Research* 54:190-208.

Blumer, H. 1936. Social attitudes and nonsymbolic interaction. *Journal of Educational Sociology* 9:515-523.

Borgstrom, G. 1965. *The Hungry Planet: The Modern World at the Edge of Famine.* New York: Macmillan Co.

Boster, M. A., R. L. Gum, and D. E. Monachi. 1973. A socio-economic analysis of Colorado River trips with policy implications. *Journal of Travel Research.* 12(1):7-10.

Boteler, F. E. 1984. Carrying capacity as a framework for managing whitewater use. *Journal of Park and Recreation Management* 2:26-36.

Brightbill, C. K. 1960. *The Challenge of Leisure.* Englewood Cliffs, N. J.: Prentice-Hall, Inc.

Brown, P. J. 1977. Information needs for river recreation planning and management. Pages 193-201 in: *Proceedings: River Recreation Management and Research Symposium.* USDA Forest Service General Technical Report NC-28.

Brown, P. J., B. L. Driver, D. H. Burns, and C. McConnell. 1979. The outdoor Recreation Opportunity Spectrum in wildland recreation planning: Development and application. Pages 1-12 in: *First Annual National Conference on Recreation Planning and Development: Proceedings of the Specialty Conference (Vol. 2).* Washington, D.C.: Society of Civil Engineers.

Brown, P. J., B. L. Driver, and C. McConnell. 1978. The opportunity spectrum concept in outdoor recreation supply inventories: Background and application. Pages 73-84 in: *Proceedings of the Integrated Renewable Resource Inventories Workshop.* USDA Forest Service General Technical Report RM-55.

Brown, P. J., A. Dyer, and R. S. Whaley. 1973. Recreation research—so what? *Journal of Leisure Research* 5(1):16-24.

Brown, P. J., and G. E. Haas. 1980. Wilderness recreation experiences: The Rawah case. *Journal of Leisure Research* 12(3):229-241.

Brown, P. J., J. E. Hautaluoma, and S. M. McPhail. 1977. Colorado deer hunting experiences. Pages 216-225 in: *Transactions of the North American Wildlife and Natural Resources Conference.* Washington, D.C.: Wildlife Management Institute.

Brown, P. J., and J. D. Hunt. 1969. The influence of information signs on visitor distribution and use. *Journal of Leisure Research* 1(1):79-83.

Brown, P. J., and D. M. Ross. 1982. Using desired recreation experiences to predict setting preferences. Pages 105-110 in: *Forest and River Recreation: Research Update.* University of Minnesota Agricultural Experiment Station Miscellaneous Report 18.

Bryan, H. 1977. Leisure value systems and recreational specialization: The case of trout fishermen. *Journal of Leisure Research* 9(3):174-187.

Buchanan, T., J. E. Christensen, and R. J. Burdge. 1981. Social groups and the meanings of outdoor recreation activities. *Journal of Leisure Research* 13(3):254-266.

Buist, L. J., and T. A. Hoots. 1982. Recreation Opportunity Spectrum approach to resource planning. *Journal of Forestry* 80(2):84-86.

Bultena, G. L., D. Albrecht, and P. Womble. 1981a. Freedom versus control: A study of backpackers preferences for wilderness management. *Leisure Sciences* 4(3):297-310.

Bultena, G. L., and D. R. Field. 1978. Visitors to national parks: A test of the elitism argument. *Leisure Sciences* 1(4):395-409.

Bultena, G. L., and D. R. Field. 1980. Structural effects in national parkgoing. *Leisure Sciences* 3(3):221-240.

Bultena, G. L., D. R. Field, P. Womble, and D. Albrecht. 1981b. Closing the gates: A study of backcountry use-limitation at Mount McKinley National Park. *Leisure Sciences* 4(3):249-267.

Bultena, G. L., and L. L. Klessig. 1969. Satisfaction in camping: A conceptualization and guide to social research. *Journal of Leisure Research* 1(Aut.):348-364.

Bultena, G. L., and M. J. Taves. 1961. Changing wilderness images and forest policy. *Journal of Forestry* 59(3):167-171.

Burch, W. R., Jr. 1964. Two concepts for guiding recreation decisions. *Journal of Forestry* 62:707-712.

Burch, W. R., Jr. 1965. The play world of camping: Research into the social meaning of outdoor recreation. *American Journal of Sociology* 70(5):604-612.

Burch, W. R., Jr. 1966. Wilderness—The life cycle and forest recreational choice. *Journal of Forestry* 64:606-610.

Burch, W. R., Jr. 1969. The social circles of leisure: Competing explanations. *Journal of Leisure Research* 1(2):125-147.

Burch, W. R., Jr. 1974. In democracy is the preservation of wilderness. *Appalachia* 40(2):90-101.

Burch, W. R., Jr. 1981. The ecology of metaphor—Spacing regularities for humans and other primates in urban and wildland habitats. *Leisure Sciences* 4(3):213-231.

Burch, W. R., Jr. 1984. Much Ado About Nothing—Some reflections on the wider and wilder implications of social carrying capacity. *Leisure Sciences* 6(4):487-496.

Burch, W. R., Jr., and W. D. Wenger, Jr. 1967. *The Social Characteristics of Participants in Three Styles of Family Camping.* USDA Forest Service Research Paper PNW-48.

Burdge, R. J. 1969. Levels of occupational prestige and leisure activity. *Journal of Leisure Research* 9(Sum.):262-274.

Burdge, R. J. 1974. The state of leisure research. *Journal of Leisure Research* 6(Fall):312-319.

Burdge, R. J. 1983. Making leisure and recreation research a scholarly topic: Views of a journal editor, 1972-1982. *Leisure Sciences* 6(1):99-126.

Burdge, R. J., and D. R. Field. 1972. Methodological perspectives for the study of outdoor recreation. *Journal of Leisure Research* 4(Winter):63-72.

Burdge, R. J., and J. C. Hendee. 1972. The demand survey dilemma: Assessing the credibility of state outdoor recreation plans. *Guideline* 3(6):11-18.

Bureau of Outdoor Recreation. 1972. *The 1965 Survey of Outdoor Recreation Activities.* Washington, D.C.: U.S. Government Printing Office.

Bureau of Outdoor Recreation. 1973. *Outdoor Recreation: A Legacy for America.* Washington, D.C.: U.S. Government Printing Office.

Burgess, R. L., R. N. Clark, and J. C. Hendee. 1971. An experimental analysis of anti-litter procedures. *Journal of Applied Behavior Analysis* 4(2):71-75.

Bury, R. L. 1964. *Information on Campground Use and Visitor Characteristics.* USDA Forest Service Research Note PSW-43.

Bury, R. L. 1976. Recreation carrying capacity—Hypothesis or reality? *Parks and Recreation* 11(1):23-25, 56-58.

Bury, R. L., and C. B. Fish. 1980. Controlling wilderness recreation: What managers think and do. *Journal of Soil and Water Conservation* 35(2):90-93.

Bury, R. L., and J. W. Hall. 1963. *Estimating Past and Current Attendance at Winter Sports Areas.* USDA Forest Service Research Note PSW-33.

Bury, R. L., and R. Margolis. 1964. *A Method for Estimating Current Attendance on Sets of Campgrounds.* USDA Forest Service Research Note PSW-42.

Campbell, F. L. 1970. Participant observation in outdoor recreation. *Journal of Leisure Research* 2(4):226-236.

Canon, L. K., S. P. Adler, and R. E. Leonard. 1979. *Factors Affecting Backcountry Campsite Dispersion.* USDA Forest Service Research Note NE-276.

Carhart, A. H. 1961. *Planning for America's Wildlands.* Harrisburg, Pennsylvania: The Telegraph Press.

Catton, W. R., Jr. 1969. Motivations of wilderness users. *Pulp and Paper Magazine of Canada* (Woodlands Section), Dec. 19:121-126.

Catton, W. R., Jr. 1971. The wildland recreation boom and sociology. *Pacific Sociological Review* 14(July):339-357.

Chappelle, D. E. 1973. The need for outdoor recreation: An economic conundrum? *Journal of Leisure Research* 5(Fall):47-53.

Cheek, N. H., Jr. 1971. Toward a sociology of not-work. *Pacific Sociological Review* 14:245-258.

Cheek, N. H., Jr., and W. R. Burch, Jr. 1976. *The Social Organization of Leisure in Human Society.* New York: Harper and Row.

Cheek, N. H., Jr., D. R. Field, and R. J. Burdge. 1976. *Leisure and Recreation Places.* Ann Arbor, Michigan: Ann Arbor Science.

Chilman, K. C., L. F. Marnell, and D. Foster. 1981. Putting river research to work: A carrying capacity strategy. Pages 56-61 in: *Some Recent Products of River Recreation Research.* USDA Forest Service General Technical Report NC-63.

Christensen, H. H. 1981. *Bystander Intervention and Litter Control: An Experimental Analysis of an Appeal to Help Program.* USDA Forest Service Research Paper PNW-287.

Christensen, H. H., and R. N. Clark. 1983. Increasing public involvement to reduce depreciative behavior in recreation settings. *Leisure Sciences* 5(4):359-378.

Christensen, J. E., and D. R. Yoesting. 1973. Social and attitudinal variants in high and low use of outdoor recreational facilities. *Journal of Leisure Research* 5(Spr.):6-15.

Christensen, J. E., and D. R. Yoesting. 1977. The substitutability concept: A need for further development. *Journal of Leisure Research* 9(3):188-207.

Cicchetti, C. E. 1976. *The Costs of Congestion.* Cambridge, Massachusetts: Ballinger Publishing Company.

Cicchetti, C. E., J. Seneca, and P. Davidson. 1969. *The Demand and Supply of Outdoor Recreation.* New Brunswick, New Jersey: Rutgers Bureau of Economic Research.

Cicchetti, C. E., and V. Smith. 1973. Congestion, quality deterioration, and optimal use: Wilderness recreation in the Spanish Peaks Primitive Area. *Social Science Research* 2(1):15-30.

Clark, R. N. 1977. Alternative strategies for studying river recreationists. In: *Proceedings: River Recreation Management and Research Symposium.* USDA Forest Service General Technical Report NC-28.

Clark, R. N. 1982. Promises and pitfalls of the ROS in resource management. *Australian Parks and Recreation* 12:9-13.

Clark, R. N., R. L. Burgess, and J. C. Hendee. 1972a. The development of anti-litter behavior in a forest campground. *Journal of Applied Behavior Analysis* 5(1):1-5.

Clark, R. N., J. C. Hendee, and R. L. Burgess. 1972b. The experimental control of littering. *Journal of Environmental Education* 4(2):22-28.

Clark, R. N., J. C. Hendee, and F. L. Campbell. 1971a. Values, behavior, and conflict in modern camping culture. *Journal of Leisure Research* 3(3):143-159.

Clark, R. N., J. C. Hendee, and F. L. Campbell. 1971b. *Depreciative Behavior in Forest Campgrounds: An Exploratory Study.* USDA Forest Service Research Paper PNW-161.

Clark, R. N., and G. H. Stankey. 1979a. *The Recreation Opportunity Spectrum: A Framework for Planning, Management, and Research.* USDA Forest Service Research Paper PNW-98.

Clark, R. N., and G. H. Stankey. 1979b. Determining the acceptability of recreational impacts: An application of the outdoor Recreation Opportunity Spectrum. Pages 32-42 in: *Recreational Impact on Wildlands.* USDA Forest Service, USDI National Park Service, R-6-001-1979.

Clarke, A. C. 1956. The use of leisure and its relation to levels of occupational prestige. *American Sociological Review* 21(3):301-307.

Clawson, M. 1959. The crisis in outdoor recreation. *American Forests* 65(3):22-31, 40-41.

Clawson, M., and J. L. Knetsch. 1963. Outdoor recreation research: Some concepts and suggested areas of study. *Natural Resources Journal* 3(2):250-275.

Clawson, M., and J. L. Knetsch. 1966. *Economics of Outdoor Recreation.* Baltimore, Maryland: Johns Hopkins University Press.

Cohen, J. L., B. Sladen, and B. Bennett. 1975. The effects of situational variables on judgements of crowding. *Sociometry* 38(2):278-281.

Cole, D. N. 1982. Controlling the spread of campsites at popular wilderness destinations. *Journal of Soil and Water Conservation* 37:291-295.

Cordell, H. K., and C. K. Sykes. 1969. *User Preferences for Developed-Site Camping.* USDA Forest Service Research Note SE-122.

Cordell, H. K., and G. A. James. 1970. *Estimating Recreation Use at Visitor Information Centers.* USDA Forest Service Research Paper SE-69.

Cordell, H. K., and G. A. James. 1972. *Visitors Preferences for Certain Physical Characteristics of Developed Campsites.* USDA Forest Service Research Paper SE-100.

Crandall, R. 1979. Social interaction, affect and leisure. *Journal of Leisure Research* 11(3):165-181.

Crandall, R. 1980. Motivations for leisure. *Journal of Leisure Research* 12(1):45-54.

Dana, S. T. 1957. *Problem Analysis: Research in Forest Recreation.* U.S. Department of Agriculture, Washington, D.C.

Dassmann, R. F. 1964. *Wildlife Biology.* New York: John Wiley and Sons.

deBettencourt, J. S., G. L. Peterson, and P. K. Wang. 1978. Managing wilderness travel: A Markov-based linear programming model. *Environment and Planning* 10:71-79.

Decker, D. J., T. L. Brown, and R. J. Gutierrez. 1980. Further insights into the multiple satisfactions approach for hunter management. *Wildlife Society Bulletin* 8(4):323-331.

deGrazia, S. 1962. *Of Time, Work and Leisure.* New York: Twentieth Century Fund, Inc.

Department of Resource Development, Michigan State University. 1962. *The Quality of Outdoor Recreation: As Evidenced by User Satisfaction.* Outdoor Recreation Resources Review Commission Study Report 5. Washington, D.C.: U. S. Government Printing Office.

Desor, J. A. 1972. Toward a psychological theory of crowding. *Journal of Personality and Social Psychology* 21:79-83.

Deutscher, I. 1966. Words and deeds: Social science and social policy. *Social Problems* 13(3):235-254.

Devall, W., and J. Harry. 1981. Who hates whom in the great outdoors: The impact of recreational specialization and technologies of play. *Leisure Sciences* 4(4):399-418.

DeVoto, B. 1953. Let's close the national parks. *Harpers* 207(1241):49-52.

Ditton, R. B., A. J. Fedler, and A. R. Graefe. 1982. Assessing recreational satisfaction among diverse participant groups. Pages 134-139 in: *Forest and River Recreation: Research Update.* University of Minnesota Agricultural Experiment Station Miscellaneous Publication 18.

Ditton, R. B., A. J. Fedler, and A. R. Graefe. 1983. Factors contributing to perceptions of recreational crowding. *Leisure Sciences* 5(4):273-288.

Ditton, R. B., T. L. Goodale, and P. K. Johnsen. 1975. A cluster analysis of activity frequency and environment variables to identify water-based recreation types. *Journal of Leisure Research* 7(4):282-295.

Ditton, R. B., A. R. Graefe, and A. J. Fedler. 1981. Recreational satisfaction at Buffalo National River: Some measurement concerns. Pages 9-17 in: *Some Recent Products of River Recreation Research*. USDA Forest Service General Technical Report NC-63.

Donald, M. N., and R. J. Havighurst. 1959. The meanings of leisure. *Social Forces* 37:355-360.

Dorfman, P. 1979. Measurement and meaning of recreation satisfaction: A case study of camping. *Environment and Behavior* 11(4):483-510.

Dottavio, F. D., J. O'Leary, and B. Koth. 1980. The social group variable in recreation participation studies. *Journal of Leisure Research* 12(4):357-367.

Dowell, L. J. 1967. Recreational pursuits of selected occupational groups. *The Research Quarterly* 38:719-722.

Downing, K., and R. N. Clark. 1979. Users' and managers' perceptions of dispersed recreation impacts: A focus on roaded forest lands. Pages 18-23 in: *Proceedings of the Wildland Recreation Impacts Conference*. USDA Forest Service, USDI National Park Service, R-6-001-1979.

Driver, B. L. 1972. Potential contributions of psychology to recreation resources management. Pages 233-248 in: *Environment and the Social Sciences: Perspectives and Applications* (J. F. Wohlwell and D. H. Carson, eds.). Washington, D.C.: American Psychological Association.

Driver, B. L. 1975. Quantification of outdoor recreationists' preferences. Pages 165-187 in: *Reseasrch, Camping and Environmental Education* (B. vanderSmissen and J. Myers, eds.) Pennsylvania State University HPER Series 11, University Park, Pennsylvania.

Driver, B. L. 1976. Toward a better understanding of the social benefits of outdoor recreation participation. Pages 163-189 in: *Proceedings of the Southern States Recreation Research Applications Workshop*. USDA Forest Service General Technical Report SE-9.

Driver, B. L., and J. Bassett. 1975. Defining conflicts among river users: A case study of Michigan's Au Sable River. *Naturalist* 26(1):19-23.

Driver, B. L., and P. J. Brown. 1975. A socio-psychological definition of recreation demand, with implications for recreation resource planning. Pages 62-88 in: *Assessing Demand for Outdoor Recreation*. Washington, D.C.: National Academy of Sciences.

Driver, B. L., and P. J. Brown. 1978. The opportunity spectrum concept in outdoor recreation supply inventories; A rationale. Pages 24-31 in: *Proceedings of the Integrated Renewable Resource Inventories Workshop*. USDA Forest Service General Technical Report RM-55.

Driver, B. L., and P. J. Brown. 1984. Contributions of behavioral scientists to recreation resource management. Pages 307-339 in: *Behavior and the National Environment* (I. Altman and J. F. Wohlwill, eds.). New York: Plenum Press.

Driver, B. L., and R. W. Cooksey. 1977. Preferred psychological outcomes of recreational fishing. Pages 27-39 in: *Proceedings of the National Sport Fishing Symposium*. Humboldt State University, Arcata, California.

Driver, B. L., and R. C. Knopf. 1976. Temporary escape: One product of sport fisheries management. *Fisheries* 1(2):21-29.

Driver, B. L., and R. C. Knopf. 1977. Personality, outdoor recreation, and expected consequences. *Environment and Behavior* 9(2):169-193.

Driver, B. L., and R. C. Knopf. 1981. Some thoughts on the quality of outdoor recreation research and other constraints on its application. Pages 85-99 in: *Social Research in National Parks and Wilderness Areas* (K. Chilman, ed.). National Park Service, Atlanta, Georgia.

Driver, B. L., and D. H. Rosenthal. 1982. *Measuring and Improving Effectiveness of Public Outdoor Recreation Programs.* USDA Forest Service, USDI Bureau of Land Management, and George Washington University.

Driver, B. L., and R. C. Tocher. 1970. Toward a behavioral interpretation of recreational engagements, with implications for planning. Pages 9-31 in: *Elements of Outdoor Recreation Planning* (B. L. Driver, ed.). Ann Arbor, Michigan: University Microfilms.

Dunn, D. R. 1970. Motorized recreation vehicles—on borrowed time. *Parks and Recreation* 5(7):10-14, 46-52.

Dustin, D. L., and L. H. McAvoy. 1982. The decline and fall of quality recreation opportunities and environments. *Environmental Ethics* 4(Spr.):49-57.

Dustin, D. L., and L. H. McAvoy. 1984. The limitation of the traffic light. *Journal of Park and Recreation Administration* 2:28-32.

Echelberger, H. E., D. H. Deiss, and D. A. Morrison. 1974. Overuse of unique recreation areas: A look at the social problems. *Journal of Soil and Water Conservation* 29(4):173-176.

Echelberger, H. E., D. Gilroy, and G. Moeller (compilers). 1983a. *Recreation Research Publication Bibliography, 1961-1982.* Washington, D.C.: USDA Forest Service.

Echelberger, H. E., R. E. Leonard, and S. P. Adler. 1983b. Designated-dispersed tentsites. *Journal of Forestry* 81(2):90-91, 105.

Echelberger, H. E., R. E. Leonard, and M. L. Hamblin. 1978. *The Trail Guide System as a Backcountry Management Tool.* USDA Forest Service Research Note NE-266.

Echelberger, H. E. and G. H. Moeller. 1977. *Use and Users of the Cranberry Backcountry in West Virginia: Insights for Eastern Backcountry Management.* USDA Forest Service Research Paper NE-363.

Elsner, G. H. 1970. Camping use—axle count relationship: Estimation with desirable properties. *Forest Science* 16:493-495.

Etzkorn, K. P. 1964. Leisure and camping: The social meaning of a form of public recreation. *Sociology and Social Research* 49:76-89.

Faris, R., and H. W. Dunham. 1965. *Mental Disorders in Urban Areas.* Chicago, Illinois: Phoenix Books.

Fazio, J. R. 1979a. *Communicating with the Wilderness User.* University of Idaho College of Forestry, Wildlife and Range Science Bulletin Number 28.

Fazio, J. R. 1979b. Agency literature as an aid to wilderness management. *Journal of Forestry* 77(2):97-98.

Fazio, J. R., and D. L. Gilbert. 1974. Mandatory wilderness permits: Some indications of success. *Journal of Forestry* 72(12):753-756.

Ferriss, A. L. 1962. *National Recreation Survey.* Outdoor Recreation Resources Review Commission Study Report 19. Washington, D.C.: U.S. Government Printing Office.

Ferriss, A. L. 1970. The social and personality correlates of outdoor recreation. *The Annals* 389(May):46-55.

Festinger, L. 1957. *A Theory of Cognitive Dissonance.* Stanford, California: Stanford University Press.

Field, D. R., and N. H. Cheek, Jr. 1974. A basis for assessing differential participation in water-based recreation. *Water Resources Bulletin* 10:1218-1227.

Field, D. R., and D. R. Johnson. 1983. The interactive process of applied research: A partnership between scientists and park and resource managers. *Journal of Park and Recreation Administration* 1(4):18-27.

Field, D. R., and J. O'Leary. 1973. Social groups as a basis for assessing participation in selected water activities. *Journal of Leisure Research* 5(1):16-25.

Fish, C. B., and R. L. Bury. 1981. Wilderness visitor management: Diversity and agency policies. *Journal of Forestry* 79(9):608-612.

Fishbein, M., and I. Ajzen. 1974. Attitudes towards objects as predictors of single and multiple behavioral criteria. *Psychological Review* 81(1):59-74.

Fisher, A. C., and J. V. Krutilla. 1972. Determination of optimal capacity of resource-based recreation facilities. *Natural Resources Journal* 12:417-444.

Fractor, D. T. 1982. Evaluating alternative methods for rationing wilderness use. *Journal of Leisure Research* 14(4):341-349.

Freedman, J. L., S. Klevansky, and P. R. Ehrlich. 1971. The effect of crowding on human task performance. *Journal of Applied Social Psychology* 1(1):7-25.

Frissell, S. S., and D. P. Duncan. 1965. Campsite preference and deterioration. *Journal of Forestry* 63(4):256-260.

Frissell, S. S., R. G. Lee, G. H. Stankey, and E. H. Zube. 1980. A framework for estimating the consequences of alternative carrying capacity levels in Yosemite Valley. *Landscape Planning* 7:151-170.

Frissell, S. S., and G. H. Stankey. 1972. Wilderness environmental quality: Search for social and ecological harmony. *Proceedings of the Society of American Foresters Annual Conference,* Washington, D.C.

Gans, H. J. 1962. Outdoor recreation and mental health. Pages 233-242 in: *Trends in American Living and Outdoor Recreation.* Outdoor Recreation Resources Review Commission Study Report 22. Washington, D.C.: U.S. Government Printing Office.

Gerstl, J. E. 1961. Leisure, taste, and occupational milieu. *Social Problems* 9(1):56-68.

Gibson, J. J. 1977. Theory of affordances. In: *Perceiving, Acting, and Knowing: Toward an Ecological Psychology* (R. E. Shaw and J. Bransford, eds.). Hillsdale, New Jersey: Lawrence Erlbaum Associates.

Gibson, J. J. 1979. *The Ecological Approach to Visual Perception.* Boston, Massachusetts: Houghton Mifflin Company.

Gilbert, G. C., G. L. Peterson, and D. W. Lime. 1972. Towards a model of travel behavior in the Boundary Waters Canoe Area. *Environment and Behavior* 4(2):131-157.

Godin, V. B., and R. E. Leonard. 1976. Guidelines for managing backcountry travel and usage. *Trends* 13:33-37.

Godin, V. B., and R. E. Leonard. 1977a. *Permit Compliance in Eastern Wilderness: Preliminary Results.* USDA Forest Service Research Note NE-238.

Godin, V. B., and R. E. Leonard. 1977b. Design capacity for backcountry recreation management planning. *Journal of Soil and Water Conservation* 32(4): 161-164.

Godschalk, D. R., and F. H. Parker. 1975. Carrying capacity: A key to environmental planning? *Journal of Soil and Water Conservation* 30(4):160-165.

Gold, S. M. 1973. *Urban Recreation Planning.* Philadelphia, Pennsylvania: Lea and Febiger.

Graefe, A. R., R. Ditton, J. Roggenbuck, and R. Schreyer. 1981. Notes on the stability of the factor structure of leisure meanings. *Leisure Sciences* 4(1):51-65.

Graefe, A. R., J. J. Vaske, and F. R. Kuss. 1984. Social carrying capacity: An integration and synthesis of twenty years of research. *Leisure Sciences* 6(4):395-431.

Gramann, J. H. 1982. Toward a behavioral theory of crowding in outdoor recreation: An evaluation and synthesis of research. *Leisure Sciences* 5(2):109-126.

Gramann, J. H., and R. Burdge. 1981. The effect of recreation goals on conflict perceptions: The case of water skiers and fishermen. *Journal of Leisure Research* 13(1):15-27.

Greenleaf, R. D., H. E. Echelberger, and R. E. Leonard. 1984. Backpacker satisfaction, expectations, and use levels in an eastern forest setting. *Journal of Park and Recreation Administration* 2:49-56.

Griffitt, W., and R. Veitch. 1971. Hot and crowded: Influence of population density and temperature on interpersonal affective behavior. *Journal of Personality and Social Psychology* 17:92-98.

Groves, D. L., and R. Wolenski. 1977. Applied recreation research: The missing link between theoretical research and the practitioner. *Journal of Environmental Systems* 7(1):59-98.

Haas, G. E., D. J. Allen, and M. J. Manfredo. 1979. Some dispersed recreation experiences and the resource settings in which they occur. Pages 21-26 in: *Assessing Amenity Resource Values.* USDA Forest Service General Technical Report RM-68.

Haas, G. E., B. L. Driver, and P. J. Brown. 1980a. Measuring wilderness recreation experiences. Pages 20-40 in: *Proceedings of the Wilderness Psychology Group,* Durham, New Hampshire.

Haas, G. E., B. L. Driver, and P. J. Brown. 1980b. A study of ski touring experiences on the White River National Forest. Pages 25-30 in: *Proceedings of the North American Symposium on Dispersed Winter Recreation.* Office of Special Programs, Education Series 2-3, University of Minnesota, St. Paul.

Hammitt, W. E. 1982. Cognitive dimensions of wilderness solitude. *Environment and Behavior* 14(4):478-493.

Hammitt, W. E. 1983. Toward an ecological approach to perceived crowding in outdoor recreation. *Leisure Sciences* 5(4):309-320.

Hammitt, W. E., and J. L. Hughes. 1984. Characteristics of winter backcountry use in Great Smoky Mountains National Park. *Environmental Management* 8(2):161-166.

Hammitt, W. E., and C. D. McDonald. 1983. Past on-site experience and its relationship to managing river recreation resources. *Forest Science* 29(2):262-266.

Hammitt, W. E., C. D. McDonald, and H. K. Cordell. 1982. Conflict perception and visitor support for management controls. Pages 45-48 in: *Forest and River Recreation: Research Update*. University of Minnesota Agricultural Experiment Station Miscellaneous Publication 18.

Hammitt, W. E., C. D. McDonald, and F. P. Noe. 1984. Use level and encounters: Important variables of perceived crowding among non-specialized recreationists. *Journal of Leisure Research* 16(1):1-9.

Hancock, H. K. 1973. Recreation preference: Its relation to user behavior. *Journal of Forestry* 71(6):336-337.

Hardin, G. 1969. The economics of wilderness. *Natural History* 78(6):20-27.

Harry, J. 1972. Socio-economic patterns of outdoor recreation use near urban areas—A comment. *Journal of Leisure Research* 4:218-219.

Hautaluoma, J. E., and P. J. Brown. 1978. Attributes of the deer hunting experience: A cluster analytic study. *Journal of Leisure Research* 10(4):271-287.

Hautaluoma, J. E., P. J. Brown, and N. L. Battle. 1982. Elk hunter consumer satisfaction patterns. Pages 74-80 in: *Forest and River Recreation: Research Update*. University of Minnesota Agricultural Experiment Station Miscellaneous Publication 18.

Havighurst, R. J., and K. Feigenbaum. 1959. Leisure and life-style. *American Journal of Sociology* 64:396-404.

Hawes, D. K. 1978. Satisfaction derived from leisure time pursuits: An exploratory nationwide survey. *Journal of Leisure Research* 10(4):247-264.

Heberlein, T. A. 1973. Social psychological assumptions of user attitude surveys: The case of the wilderness scale. *Journal of Leisure Research* 5(3):18-33.

Heberlein, T. A. 1977. Density, crowding, and satisfaction: Sociological studies for determining carrying capacities. Pages 67-76 in: *Proceedings: River Recreation Management and Research Symposium*. USDA Forest Service General Technical Report NC-28.

Heberlein, T. A., and P. Dunwiddie. 1979. Systematic observation of use levels, campsite selection and visitor characteristics at a high mountain lake. *Journal of Leisure Research* 11(4):307-316.

Heberlein, T. A., and B. Shelby. 1977. Carrying capacity, values, and the satisfaction model: A reply to Greist. *Journal of Leisure Research* 9(2):142-148.

Heberlein, T. A., J. N. Trent, and R. M. Baumgartner. 1982. The influence of hunter density on firearm deer hunters' satisfaction: A field experiment. *Transactions of the 47th North American Natural Resource and Wildlife Conference* 47:665-676.

Helgath, S. F. 1975. *Trail Deterioration in the Selway-Bitterroot Wilderness*. USDA Forest Service Research Note INT-193.

Hendee, J. C. 1971. Sociology and applied leisure research. *Pacific Sociological Review* 14:360-368.

Hendee, J. C. 1974. A multiple-satisfaction approach to game management. *Wildlife Society Bulletin* 2(3):104-113.

Hendee, J. C., and R. S. Burdge. 1974. The substitutability concept: Implications for recreation management and research. *Journal of Leisure Research* 6(2):157-162.

Hendee, J. C., W. R. Catton, Jr., L. D. Marlow, and C. F. Brockman. 1968. *Wilderness Users in the Pacific Northwest—Their Characteristics, Values and Management Preferences.* USDA Forest Service Research Paper PNW-61.

Hendee, J. C., R. W. Clark, and T. E. Daily. 1977a. *Fishing and Other Recreation Behavior at High-Mountain Lakes in Washington State.* USDA Forest Service Research Note PNW-304.

Hendee, J. C., R. P. Gale, and W. R. Catton, Jr. 1971. A typology of outdoor recreation activity preferences. *Journal of Environmental Education* 3(1):28-34.

Hendee, J. C., and R. W. Harris. 1970. Foresters' perceptions of wilderness-user attitudes and preferences. *Journal of Forestry* 68(12):759-762.

Hendee, J. C., M. L. Hogans, and R. W. Koch. 1976. *Dispersed Recreation on Three Forest Road Systems in Washington and Oregon: First Year Data.* USDA Forest Service Research Note PNW-280.

Hendee, J. C., and R. C. Lucas. 1973. Mandatory wilderness permits: A necessary management tool. *Journal of Forestry* 71(4):206-209.

Hendee, J. C., and R. C. Lucas. 1974. Police state wilderness: A comment on a comment. *Journal of Forestry* 72:100-101.

Hendee, J. C., and D. R. Potter. 1975. Hunters and hunting: Management implications of research. Pages 132-161 in: *Proceedings of the Southern States Recreation Research Applications Workshop,* Asheville, North Carolina.

Hendee, J. C., and G. H. Stankey. 1973. Biocentricity in wilderness management. *BioScience* 23(9):535-538.

Hendee, J. C., G. H. Stankey, and R. C. Lucas. 1977b. *Wilderness Management.* USDA Forest Service Miscellaneous Publication 1365.

Heritage Conservation and Recreation Service. 1979. *The Third Nationwide Outdoor Recreation Plan.* Washington, D.C.: U.S. Government Printing Office.

Hogans, M. L. 1978. *Using Photography for Recreation Research.* USDA Forest Service Research Note PNW-327.

Hollandar, J. 1977. Motivational dimensions of the camping experience. *Journal of Leisure Research* 9(2):133-141.

Howard, D. R. 1976. Multivariate relationships between leisure activities and personality. *Research Quarterly* 47:226-237.

Hulbert, J. H., and J. F. Higgans. 1977. BWCA visitor distribution system. *Journal of Forestry* 75:338-340.

Hunt, S. L., and K. W. Brooks. 1983. A planning model for public recreation agencies. *Journal of Park and Recreation Administration* 1(2):1-12.

Iso-Ahola, S., and J. Allen. 1982. The dynamics of leisure motivation: The effects of outcome on leisure needs. *Research Quarterly* 53(2):141-149.

Jackson, E. L., and R. A. G. Wong. 1982. Perceived conflict between urban cross-country skiers and snowmobilers in Alberta. *Journal of Leisure Research* 14(1):47-62.

Jacob, G. R., and R. Schreyer. 1980. Conflict in outdoor recreation: A theoretical perspective. *Journal of Leisure Research* 12(4):368-380.

James, G. A. 1968. *Pilot Test of Sampling Procedures for Estimating Recreation Use on Winter Sports Sites.* USDA Forest Service Research Paper SE-42.

James, G. A. 1971. Inventorying recreation use. Pages 78-95 in: *Recreation Symposium Proceedings*. USDA Forest Service.

James, G. A., and H. K. Cordell. 1970. *Importance of Shading to Visitors Selecting a Campsite at Indian Boundary Campground in Tennessee*. USDA Forest Service Research Note SE-130.

James, G. A., and R. W. Henley. 1968. *Sampling Procedures for Estimating Mass and Dispersed Types of Recreation Use on Large Areas*. USDA Forest Service Research Paper SE-31.

James, G. A., and A. K. Quinkert. 1972. *Estimating Recreational Use at Developed Observation Sites*. USDA Forest Service Research Paper SE-97.

James, G. A., and J. L. Rich. 1966. *Estimating Recreation Use on a Complex of Developed Sites*. USDA Forest Service Research Note SE-64.

James, G. A., and T. H. Ripley. 1963. *Instructions for Using Traffic Counters to Estimate Recreation Visits and Use*. USDA Forest Service Research Paper SE-3.

James, G. A., and H. T. Schreuder. 1971. Estimating recreation use in the San Gorgonio Wilderness. *Journal of Forestry* 69(8):490-493.

James, G. A., and H. T. Schreuder. 1972. *Estimating Dispersed Recreation Use Along Trails and in General Undeveloped Areas with Electric-Eye Counters: Some Preliminary Findings*. USDA Forest Service Research Note SE-181.

James, G. A., N. W. Taylor, and M. L. Hopkins. 1971a. *Estimating Recreational Use of a Unique Trout Stream in the Coastal Plains of South Carolina*. USDA Forest Service Research Note SE-159.

James, G. A., and G. L. Tyre. 1967. *Use of Water-Meter Records to Estimate Recreation Visits and Use on Developed Sites*. USDA Forest Service Research Note SE-73.

James, G. A., H. P. Wingle, and J. D. Griggs. 1971b. *Estimating Recreation Use on Large Bodies of Water*. USDA Forest Service Research Paper SE-79.

Johnson, D., and D. R. Field. 1981. Applied and basic social research: A difference in social context. *Leisure Sciences* 4(3):269-279.

Jubenville, A. 1971. A test of difference between wilderness recreation party leaders and party members. *Journal of Leisure Research* 3(2):116-119.

Jubenville, A., and R. H. Becker. 1983. Outdoor recreation management planning: Contemporary schools of thought. Pages 303-319 in: *Recreation Planning and Management* (S. R. Lieber and D. R. Fesenmaier, eds.). State College, Pennsylvania: Venture Publishing Company.

Kaplan, M. 1960. *Leisure in America: A Social Inquiry*. New York: John Wiley and Sons, Inc.

Kaplan, R. 1974. Some psychological benefits of an outdoor challenge program. *Environment and Behavior* 6:101-116.

Kelly, J. R. 1974. Socialization toward leisure: A developmental approach. *Journal of Leisure Research* 6:181-193.

Kelly, J. R. 1980. Outdoor recreation participation: A comparative analysis. *Leisure Sciences* 3(2):129-154.

King, D. A. 1965. *Characteristics of Family Campers Using the Huron-Manistee National Forests*. USDA Forest Service Research Paper LS-19.

King, D. A. 1966. *Activity Patterns of Campers*. USDA Forest Service Research Note NC-18.

King, D. A. 1968. Socioeconomic variables related to campsite use. *Forest Science* 14(March):45-54.

Klukas, R., and D. P. Duncan. 1967. Vegetation preferences among Itasca Park visitors. *Journal of Forestry* 65(1):18-21.

Knetsch, J. L. 1969. Assessing the demand for outdoor recreation. *Journal of Leisure Research* 1:83-94.

Knopf, R. C., and J. D. Barnes. 1980. Determinants of satisfaction with a tourist resource: A case study of visitors to Gettysburg National Military Park. Pages 217-233 in: *Tourism Marketing and Management Issues*. Washington, D.C.: George Washington University.

Knopf, R. C., B. L. Driver, and J. R. Bassett. 1973. Motivations for fishing. Pages 28-41 in: *Human Dimensions in Wildlife Programs*. The Wildlife Management Institute, Washington, D.C.

Knopf, R. C., and D. W. Lime. 1981. *The National River Recreation Study Questionnaires: An Aid to Recreation Management*. USDA Forest Service Research Paper NC-222.

Knopf, R. C., and D. W. Lime. 1984. *A Recreation Manager's Guide to Understanding River Use and Users*. USDA Forest Service General Technical Report WO-38.

Knopf, R. C., G. L. Peterson, and E. C. Leatherberry. 1983. Motives of recreational river floating: Relative consistency across settings. *Leisure Sciences* 5(3):231-255.

Knopp, T., G. Ballman, and L. C. Merriam, Jr. 1979. Toward a more direct measure of river user preferences. *Journal of Leisure Research* 11(4):317-326.

Knopp, T., and J. Tyger. 1973. A study of conflict in recreational land use: Snowmobiling vs. ski-touring. *Journal of Leisure Research* 5:6-17.

Knudson, D. M., and E. B. Curry. 1981. Campers' perceptions of site deterioration and crowding. *Journal of Forestry* 79:92-94.

Krumpe, E. E., and P. J. Brown. 1982. Redistributing backcountry use through information related to recreational experiences. *Journal of Forestry* 80(6):360-362.

Krutilla, J. V. 1967. Conservation reconsidered. *American Economic Review* 57(4):777-786.

LaPage, W. F. 1963. Some sociological aspects of forest recreation. *Journal of Forestry* 61(1):32-36.

LaPage W. F. 1967. *Camper Characteristics Differ at Public and Commercial Campgrounds in New England*. USDA Forest Service Research Note NE-59.

LaPage, W. F. 1973. *Growth Potential of the Family Camping Market*. USDA Forest Service Research Paper NE-252.

LaPage, W. F. (Compiler). 1980. *Proceedings: 1980 National Outdoor Recreation Trends Symposium*. USDA Forest Service General Technical Report NE-57 (2 Vols.).

LaPage, W. F. 1983. Recreation resource management for visitor satisfaction. Pages 279-285 in: *Recreation Planning and Management* (S. R. Lieber and D. R. Fesenmaier, eds.). State College, Pennsylvania: Venture Publishing Company.

LaPage, W. F., and M. I. Bevins. 1981. *Satisfaction Monitoring for Quality Control in Campground Management*. USDA Forest Service Research Paper NE-484.

LaPage, W. F., P. L. Cormier, G. T. Hamilton, and A. D. Cormier. 1975. *Differential Campsite Pricing and Campground Attendance.* USDA Forest Service Research Paper NE-330.

LaPage, W. F., and D. P. Ragain. 1974. Family camping trends—An eight-year panel study. *Journal of Leisure Research* 6(Spr.):101-112.

Larrabee, E., and R. Meyersohn (eds.) 1958. *Mass Leisure.* Glencoe, Illinois: The Free Press.

Lawler, E. E. 1973. *Motivations in Work Organizations.* Monterey, California: Brooks/Cole Publishing Company.

Leatherberry, E. C., and D. W. Lime. 1981. *Unstaffed Trail Registration Compliance in a Backcountry Recreation Area.* USDA Forest Service Research Paper NC-214.

Lee, R. G. 1972. The social definition of outdoor recreation places. Pages 68-84 in: *Social Behavior, Natural Resources, and the Environment* (W. R. Burch, N. H. Cheek, and L. Taylor, eds.). New York: Harper and Row.

Lee, R. G. 1975. *The Management of Human Components in the Yosemite National Park Ecosystem: Final Research Report.* Berkeley, California; University of California.

Lee, R. G. 1977. Alone with others: The paradox of privacy in wilderness. *Leisure Sciences* 1(1):3-19.

Leonard, R. E., H. E. Echelberger, H. J. Plumley, and L. W. VanMeter. 1980. *Management Guidelines for Monitoring Use on Backcountry Trails.* USDA Forest Service Research Note NE-286.

Leonard, R. E., H. E. Echelberger, and M. Schnitzer. 1978. *Use Characteristics of the Great Gulf Wilderness.* USDA Forest Service Research Paper NE-428.

Leopold, A. 1934. Conservation economics. *Journal of Forestry* 32:537-544.

Levitt, L. 1982. How effective is wilderness therapy? A critical review. Pages 81-93 in: *Proceedings of the Wilderness Psychology Group Conference,* West Virginia University, Morgantown.

Librarian of Congress. 1962. *Outdoor Recreation Literature: A Survey.* Outdoor Recreation Resources Review Commission Study Report 27. Washington, D.C.: U.S. Government Printing Office.

Lime, D. W. 1971. *Factors Influencing Campground Use in the Superior National Forest of Minnesota.* USDA Forest Service Research Paper NC-60.

Lime, D. W. 1972a. Behavioral research in outdoor recreation management: An example of how visitors select campgrounds. Pages 198-206 in: *Environment and the Social Sciences: Perspectives and Applications* (J. F. Wohlwill and D. H. Carson, eds.). Washington, D.C.: American Psychological Association.

Lime, D. W. 1972b. *Large Groups in the Boundary Waters Canoe Area—Their Numbers, Characteristics, and Impact.* USDA Forest Service Research Note NC-142.

Lime, D. W. 1976. Wilderness use and users: A summary of research. In: *Proceedings of the 54th Annual Winter Meeting,* Allegheny Section, Society of American Foresters, Dover, Delaware.

Lime, D. W. 1977a. Principles of recreation carrying capacity. Pages 122-134 in: *Proceedings of the Southern States Recreation Research Applications Workshop,* Asheville, North Carolina.

Lime, D. W. 1977b. When the wilderness gets crowded . . .? *Naturalist* 28(4):1-7.

Lime, D. W. 1977c. Alternative strategies for visitor management of western whitewater river recreation. Pages 146-169 in: *Managing Colorado River Whitewater: The Carrying Capacity Strategy.* Logan, Utah: Utah State University

Lime, D. W. 1979. Carrying capacity. *Trends* 16(2):37-40.

Lime, D. W., and R. Buchman. 1974. Putting wilderness permit information to work. *Journal of Forestry* 72(10):622-626.

Lime, D. W., R. C. Knopf, and G. L. Peterson. 1981. The National River Recreation Study: Growing new data base with exciting potential. In: *Some Recent Products of River Recreation Research*, USDA Forest Service General Technical Report NC-63.

Lime, D. W., and G. A. Lorence. 1974. *Improving Estimates of Wilderness Use From Mandatory Travel Permits.* USDA Forest Service Research Paper NC-101.

Lime, D. W., and R. C. Lucas. 1977. Good information improves the wilderness experience. *Naturalist* 28(4):18-20.

Lime, D. W., and G. H. Stankey. 1971. Carrying capacity: Maintaining outdoor recreation quality. Pages 174-184 in: *Recreation Symposium Proceedings.* USDA Forest Service.

Lindsay, J. J., and R. A. Ogle. 1972. Socioeconomic patterns of outdoor recreation use near urban areas. *Journal of Leisure Research* 4(Winter):19-24.

Lloyd, R. D. and V. L. Fischer. 1972. Dispersed versus concentrated recreation as forest policy. Paper presented at the Seventh World Forestry Congress, Buenos Aires, Argentina.

London, M., R. Crandall, and D. Fitzgibbons. 1977. The psychological structure of leisure: Activities, needs, people. *Journal of Leisure Research* 9(4):252-263.

Lottier, S. 1938. Distribution of criminal offenses in metropolitan regions. *Journal of Criminal Law and Criminology* 29:39-45.

Love, L. D. 1964. *Summer Recreational Use of Selected National Forest Campgrounds in the Central Rocky Mountains.* USDA Forest Service Research Paper RM-5.

Lucas, R. C. 1964a. *Recreational Use of the Quetico-Superior Area.* USDA Forest Service Research Paper LS-8.

Lucas, R. C. 1964b. *The Recreational Capacity of the Quetico-Superior Area.* USDA Forest Service Research Paper LS-15.

Lucas, R. C. 1964c. Wilderness perception and use: The example of the Boundary Waters Canoe Area. *Natural Resources Journal* 3(3):394-411.

Lucas, R. C. 1966. The contribution of environmental research to wilderness policy decisions. *Journal of Social Issues* 22(Oct.):117-126.

Lucas, R. C. 1970. *User Evaluation of Campgrounds on Two Michigan National Forests.* USDA Forest Service Research Paper NC-44.

Lucas, R. C. 1973. Wilderness: A management framework. *Journal of Soil and Water Conservation* 28(4):150-154.

Lucas, R. C. 1975. *Low Compliance Rates at Unmanned Trail Registers.* USDA Forest Service Research Note INT-200.

Lucas, R. C. 1979. Perceptions of non-motorized recreational impacts: A review of research findings. Pages 24-31 in: *Recreational Impact on Wildlands.* USDA Forest Service, USDI National Park Service, R-6-001-1979.

Lucas, R. C. 1980. *Use Patterns and Visitor Characteristics, Attitudes, and Preferences in Nine Wilderness and Other Roadless Areas.* USDA Forest Service Research Paper INT-253.

Lucas, R. C. 1981. *Redistributing Wilderness Use Through Information Supplied to Visitors.* USDA Forest Service Research Paper INT-277.

Lucas, R. C. 1982a. The role of regulations in recreation management. *Western Wildlands* 8:6-10.

Lucas, R. C. 1982b. Recreation regulations—when are they needed? *Journal of Forestry* 80:148-151.

Lucas, R. C., and T. J. Kovalicky. 1981. *Self-Issued Wilderness Permits as a Use Measurement System.* USDA Forest Service Research Paper INT-270.

Lucas, R. C., and J. Oltman. 1971. Survey sampling wilderness visitors. *Journal of Leisure Research* 3(1):28-43.

Lucas, R. C., H. T. Schreuder, and G. A. James. 1971. *Wilderness Use Estimation: A Pilot Test of Sampling Procedures on the Mission Mountains Primitive Area.* USDA Forest Service Research Paper INT-109.

Lucas, R. C., and G. H. Stankey. 1974. Social carrying capacity for backcountry recreation. Pages 14-23 in: *Outdoor Recreation Research: Applying the Results.* USDA Forest Service General Technical Report NC-9.

Lundberg, G. A., M. Komarovsky, and M. A. McInerny. 1934. *Leisure: A Suburban Study.* New York: Columbia University Press.

Lynd, R. S., and H. M. Lynd. 1929. *Middletown, A Study in American Culture.* New York: Harcourt Brace.

MacDonald, M., C. McGuire, and R. J. Havighurst. 1949. Leisure activities and the socioeconomic status of children. *American Journal of Sociology* 54:505-519.

Manfredo, M. J. 1984. The comparability of onsite and offsite measures of recreation needs. *Journal of Leisure Research* 16(3):245-249.

Manfredo, M. J., B. L. Driver, and P. J. Brown. 1983. A test of concepts inherent in experience based setting management for outdoor recreation areas. *Journal of Leisure Research* 15(3):263-283.

Manning, R. E. 1979. Strategies for managing recreational use of national parks. *Parks* 4(1):13-15.

Manning, R. E. 1985. Diversity in a democracy: Expanding the Recreation Opportunity Spectrum. *Leisure Sciences* 7(4):376-398.

Manning, R. E., E. A. Callinan, H. E. Echelberger, E. J. Koenemann, and D. N. McEwen. 1984. Differential fees: Raising revenue, distributing demand. *Journal of Park and Recreation Administration* 2(1):20-38.

Manning, R. E., and C. P. Ciali. 1980. Recreation density and user satisfaction: A further exploration of the satisfaction model. *Journal of Leisure Research* 12(4):329-345.

Manning, R. E., and C. P. Ciali. 1981. Recreation and river type: Social-environmental relationships. *Environmental Management* 5(2):109-120.

Manning, R. E., and P. L. Cormier. 1980. Trends in the temporal distribution of park use. Pages 81-87 in: *Proceedings of the 1980 Outdoor Recreation Trends Symposium, Volume II.* USDA Forest Service General Technical Report NE-57.

Manning, R. E., and F. I. Potter. 1984. Computer simulation as a tool in teaching park and wilderness management. *Journal of Environmental Education*.

Manning, R. E., and L. A. Powers. 1984. Peak and off-peak use: Redistributing the outdoor recreation/tourism load. *Journal of Travel Research* 23(2):25-31.

Manning, R. E., L. A. Powers, and C. E. Mock. 1982. Temporal distribution of forest recreation; Problems and potential. Pages 26-32 in: *Forest and River Recreation: Research Update*. University of Minnesota Agricultural Experiment Station Miscellaneous Publication 18.

Marcin, T. C., and D. W. Lime. 1977. Our changing population structure: What will it mean for future outdoor recreation use? Pages 42-53 in: *Outdoor Recreation: Advances in the Application of Economics*. USDA Forest Service General Technical Report WO-2.

Marnell, L. F. 1977. Methods for counting river recreation users. Pages 77-82 in *Proceedings: River Recreation Management and Research Symposium*. USDA Forest Service General Technical Report NC-28.

Marshall, N. J. 1972. Privacy and environment. *Human Ecology* 1:93-110.

Marshall, N. J. 1974. Dimensions of privacy preferences. *Multivariate Behavioral Research* 9(July):255-272.

Maslow, A. H. 1943. A theory of human motivation. *Psychological Review* 50:370-396.

McAvoy, L. H., and D. L. Dustin. 1983. Indirect versus direct regulation of recreation behavior. *Journal of Park and Recreation Administration* 1(4):12-17.

McCay, R. E., and G. H. Moeller. 1976. *Compatibility of Ohio Trail Users*. USDA Forest Service Research Note NE-225.

McConnell, K. E. 1977. Congestion and willingness to pay: A study of beach use. *Land Economics* 53(May):185-195.

McCool, S. F., D. W. Lime, and D. H. Anderson. 1977. Simulation modeling as a tool for managing river recreation. Pages 304-311 in: *Proceedings: River Recreation Management and Research Symposium*. USDA Forest Service General Technical Report NC-28.

McCool, S. F., and R. M. Schreyer. 1977. Research utilization in wildland recreation management: A preliminary analysis. *Journal of Leisure Research* 9(2):98-109.

McCool, S. F., and J. Utter. 1981. Preferences for allocating river recreation use. *Water Resources Bulletin* 17(3):431-437.

McKechnie, G. E. 1974. The psychological structure of leisure: Past behavior. *Journal of Leisure Research* 6(1):27-45.

McLaughlin, W. J., and W. E. J. Paradice. 1980. Using visitor preference information to guide dispersed winter recreation management for cross-country skiing and snowmobiling. Pages 64-70 in: *Proceedings of the North American Symposium on Dispersed Winter Recreation*. Office of Special Programs, Education Series 2-3, University of Minnesota, St. Paul.

Meadows, D. H., D. L. Meadows, J. Randers, and W. W. Behrens III. 1972. *The Limits to Growth*. New York: Universe Books.

Meinecke, E. P. 1928. *A Report upon the Effects of Excessive Tourist Travel on the California Redwood Parks*. Sacramento, California: California State Printing Office.

Merriam, L. C., Jr., and R. B. Ammons. 1968. Wilderness users and management in three Montana areas. *Journal of Forestry* 66(5):390-395.

Merriam, L. C., Jr., and C. K. Smith. 1974. Visitor impact on newly developed campsites in the Boundary Waters Canoe Area. *Journal of Forestry* 72(10):627-630.

Merriam, L. C., Jr., K. D. Wald, and C. E. Ramsey. 1972. Public and professional definitions of the state park: A Minnesota case. *Journal of Leisure Research* 4(Fall):259-274.

Meyersohn, R. 1969. The sociology of leisure in the United States: Introduction and bibliography, 1945-1965. *Journal of Leisure Research* 1(1):53-68.

Milgram, S. 1970. The experience of living in cities. *Science* 167(Mar.):1461-1468.

Miller, R. R., A. Prato, and R. A. Young. 1977. Congestion, success, and the value of Colorado deer hunting experiences. Pages 129-136 in: *Transactions of the Forty-Second North American Wildlife and Natural Resources Conference*. Wildlife Management Institute, Washington, D.C.

Mitchell, L. S. 1969. Recreational geography: Evolution and research needs. *Professional Geographer* 21:117-119.

Mitchell, R. 1971. Some social implications of higher density housing. *American Sociological Review* 36:18-29.

Moeller, G. H., and J. H. Engelken. 1972. What fishermen look for in a fishing experience. *Journal of Wildlife Management* 36:1253-1257.

Moeller, G. H., R. G. Larson, and D. A. Morrison. 1974. *Opinions of Campers and Boaters at the Allegheny Reservoir*. USDA Forest Service Research Paper NE-307.

Moncrief, L. W. 1970. Trends in outdoor recreation research. *Journal of Leisure Research* 2(2):127-130.

More, T. A. 1980. *Trail Deterioration as an Indicator of Trail Use in an Urban Forest Recreation Area*. USDA Forest Service Research Note NE-292.

More, T. A., and G. Buhyoff. 1979. *Managing Recreation Areas for Quality Experiences: A Theoretical Framework*. USDA Forest Service Research Paper NE-432.

Moss, W. T., and S. C. Lamphear. 1970. Substitutability of recreational activities in meeting stated needs and drives of the visitor. *Environmental Education* 1(4):129-131.

Moss, W. T., L. Shackelford, and G. L. Stokes. 1969. Recreation and personality. *Journal of Forestry* 67:182-184.

Mueller, E., and G. Gurin. 1962. *Participation in Outdoor Recreation: Factors Affecting Demand Among American Adults*. Outdoor Recreation Resources Review Commission Study Report 20. Washington, D.C.: U.S. Government Printing Office.

Munley, V. G., and V. K. Smith. 1976. Learning-by-doing and experience: The case of whitewater recreation. *Land Economics* 52(4):545-553.

Murray, J. B. 1974. *Appalachian Trail Users in the Southern National Forests: Their Characteristics, Attitudes, and Management Preferences*. USDA Forest Service Research Paper SE-116.

Muth, R. M., and R. N. Clark. 1978. *Public Participation in Wilderness and Backcountry Litter Control: A Review of Research and Management Experience*. USDA Forest Service General Technical Report PNW-75.

National Academy of Sciences. 1969. *A Program for Outdoor Recreation Research*. Washington, D.C.

Neulinger, J., and M.- Breit. 1969. Attitude dimensions of leisure. *Journal of Leisure Research* 1:255-261.

Neulinger, J., and M. Breit. 1971. Attitude dimensions of leisure: A replication study. *Journal of Leisure Research* 3(2):108-115.

Neumeyer, M. H., and E. S. Neumeyer. 1949. *Leisure and Recreation.* New York: A. S. Barnes and Company.

Nielson, J. M., and R. Endo. 1977. Where have all the purists gone? An empirical examination of the displacement hypothesis in wilderness recreation. *Western Sociological Review* 8(1):61-75.

Nielson, J. M., and B. Shelby. 1977. River-running in the Grand Canyon: How much and what kind of use. Pages 168-177 in: *Proceedings: River Recreation Management and Research Symposium.* USDA Forest Service General Technical Report NC-28.

Nielson, J. M., B. Shelby, and J. E. Haas. 1977. Sociological carrying capacity and the last settler syndrome. *Pacific Sociological Review* 20(4):568-581.

Noe, F. P., R. B. Hull, and J. D. Wellman. 1982. Normative response and norm activation among ORV users within a seashore environment. *Leisure Sciences* 5(2):127-142.

Noe, F. P., J. O. Wellman, and G. J. Buhyoff. 1981. Perception of conflict between off-road vehicle users in a leisure setting. *Journal of Environmental Systems* 11(3):243-253.

Odum, E. P. 1959. *Fundamentals of Biology.* Philadelphia: W. B. Saunders Company.

O'Leary, J. T., D. Field, and G. Schreuder. 1974. Social groups and water activity clusters: An exploration of interchangeability and substitutions. Pages 195-215 in: *Water and Community Development: Social and Economic Perspectives* (J. C. Baron and B. Long, eds.). Ann Arbor: Ann Arbor Science Publishers, Inc.

O'Leary, J. T., and G. Pate. 1979. Water-based activity involvement for recreation consumers at state, federal, local, or private facilities. *Water Resources Bulletin* 15(1):182-188.

O'Leary, J. T., and H. P. Weeks. 1979. Using recreation consumer data in developing wildlife management strategies. *Wildlife Society Bulletin* 7(2):98-103.

Ormrod, R. K., and R. G. Trahan. 1977. Can signs help visitors control their own behavior? *Trends* 12:25-27.

Outdoor Recreation Resources Review Commission. 1962. *Outdoor Recreation for America.* Washington, D.C.: U.S. Government Printing Office.

Parsons, D. J., T. J. Stohlgren, and P. A. Fodor. 1982. Establishing backcountry use quotas: An example from Mineral King, California. *Environmental Management* 5(4):335-340.

Parsons, D. J., T. J. Stohlgren, and J. M. Kraushaar. 1982. Wilderness permit accuracy: Differences between reported and actual use. *Environmental Management* 6(4):329-335.

Pastalan, L. A. 1970. Privacy as a behavioral concept. *Social Forces* 45:93-97.

Petersen, M. 1981. *Trends in Recreational Use of National Forest Wilderness.* USDA Forest Service Research Paper INT-319.

Peterson, G. L. 1974. A comparison of the sentiments and perceptions of canoeists and wilderness managers in the Boundary Waters Canoe Area. *Journal of Leisure Research* 6:194-206.

Peterson, G. L., and J. S. deBettencourt. 1979. Flow metering of wilderness travel in the Quetico-Superior: New findings and research needs. *Modeling and Simulation* 10:1335-1340.

Peterson, G. L., J. S. deBettencourt, and P. K. Wang. 1977. A Markov-based linear programming model of travel in the Boundary Waters Canoe Area. Pages 342-350 in: *Proceedings: River Recreation Management and Research Symposium.* USDA Forest Service General Technical Report NC-28.

Peterson, G. L., and D. W. Lime. 1973. Two sources of bias in the measurement of human response to the wilderness environment. *Journal of Leisure Research* 5(Spr.):66-73.

Peterson, G. L., and D. W. Lime. 1979. People and their behavior: A challenge for recreation management. *Journal of Forestry* 77(6):343-346.

Peterson, G. L., and D. W. Lime. 1980. Recreation policy analysis in wilderness management: A case study of the Quetico-Superior. Pages 4-13 in: *Proceedings of the Third Annual Applied Geography Conference.* Kent State University, Kent, Ohio.

Peterson, G. L., and D. W. Lime. 1978. A research-management partnership grows in Minnesota's canoe country. *Naturalist* 14:5-11.

Peterson, G. L., and E. S. Newmann. 1969. Modeling and predicting human responses to the visual recreation environment. *Journal of Leisure Research* 1(Summer):219-238.

Pfister, R. E. 1977. Campsite choice behavior in the river setting: A pilot study on the Rogue River, Oregon. Pages 351-358 in: *Proceedings: River Recreation Management and Research Symposium.* USDA Forest Service General Technical Report NC-28.

Pierce, R. C. 1980a. Dimensions of leisure. I. Satisfactions. *Journal of Leisure Research* 12(1):5-19.

Pierce, R. C. 1980b. Dimensions of leisure. II. Descriptions. *Journal of Leisure Research* 12(2):150-163.

Pierce, R. C. 1980c. Dimensions of leisure. III. Characteristics. *Journal of Leisure Research* 12(3):273-284.

Plager, A., and P. Womble. 1981. Compliance with backcountry permits in Mount McKinley National Park. *Journal of Forestry* 79(Mar.):155-156.

Plumley, H. J., H. T. Peet, and R. E. Leonard. 1978. *Records of Backcountry Use Can Assist Trail Managers.* USDA Forest Service Research Paper NE-414.

Potter, D. R., J. C. Hendee, and R. N. Clark. 1973. Hunting satisfaction: Game, guns, or nature. Pages 62-71 in: *Human Dimensions in Wildlife Programs.* The Wildlife Management Institute, Washington, D.C.

Potter, F. I., and R. E. Manning. 1984. Application of the wilderness travel simulation model to the Appalachian Trail in Vermont. *Environmental Management* 8(6):543-550.

Propst, D. B., and D. W. Lime. 1982. How satisfying is satisfaction research? Pages 124-133 in: *Forest and River Recreation: Research Update.* University of Minnesota Agricultural Experiment Station Miscellaneous Publication 18.

Rapoport, A. 1975. Toward a redefinition of density. *Environment and Behavior* 7:133-158.

Reissman, L. 1954. Class, leisure, and social participation. *American Sociological Review* 19:76-84.

Riddick, C. C., M. DeSchriver, and E. Weissinger. 1984. A methodological review of research in *Journal of Leisure Research* from 1978 to 1982. *Journal of Leisure Research* 16(4):311-321.

Ritchie, J. R. B. 1975. On the derivation of leisure activity types—A perceptual mapping approach. *Journal of Leisure Research* 7(2):128-140.

Robertson, R. D. 1982. Visitor knowledge affects visitor behavior. Pages 49-51 in: *Forest and River Recreation: Research Update.* University of Minnesota Agricultural Experiment Station Miscellaneous Report 18.

Roggenbuck, J. W., and D. L. Berrier. 1981. Communications to disperse wilderness campers. *Journal of Forestry* 75(5):295-297.

Roggenbuck, J. W., and D. L. Berrier. 1982. A comparison of the effectiveness of two communication strategies in dispersing wilderness campers. *Journal of Leisure Research* 14(1):77-89.

Roggenbuck, J. W., and R. M. Schreyer. 1977. Relations between river trip motives and perception of crowding, management preference, and experience satisfaction. Pages 359-364 in: *Proceedings: River Recreation Management and Research Symposium.* USDA Forest Service General Technical Report NC-28.

Romesburg, H. C. 1974. Scheduling models for wilderness recreation. *Journal of Environmental Management* 4(2):159-177.

Romsa, G. 1973. A method of deriving outdoor recreational activity patterns. *Journal of Leisure Research* 5(1):34-46.

Rosenthal, D. H., and B. L. Driver. 1983. Managers' perceptions of experiences sought by ski tourers. *Journal of Forestry* 81(2):88-90, 105.

Rosenthal, D. H., D. A. Waldman, and B. L. Driver. 1982. Construct validity of instruments measuring recreationists' preferences. *Leisure Sciences* 5(2):89-108.

Ross, T. L., and G. H. Moeller. 1974. *Communicating Rules in Recreation Areas.* USDA Forest Service Research Paper NE-297.

Rossman, B., and Z. Ulehla. 1977. Psychological reward values associated with wilderness use: A functional-reinforcement approach. *Environment and Behavior* 9(1):41-46.

Sargent, S. 1967. Reaction to frustration—A critique and hypothesis. Pages 151-156 in: *Readings in Psychology: Understanding Human Behavior* (J. Dyal, ed.). New York: McGraw-Hill.

Sawrey, J. 1970. *Frustration and Conflict.* Dubuque, Iowa: William C. Brown.

Sawrey, J., and C. Telford. 1975. *Adjustment and Personality.* Boston: Allyn and Bacon, Inc.

Schmitz-Scherzer, R., G. Rudinger, A. Anglemer, and D. Bierhoff-Altermann. 1974. Notes on a factor analysis comparative study of the structure of leisure activities in four different samples. *Journal of Leisure Research* 6(1):77-83.

Schoenfeld, C. S. 1976. Who's minding the wilderness store? *Journal of Soil and Water Conservation* 31:242-247.

Schomaker, J. H., and R. C. Knopf. 1982a. Effect of question context on a recreation satisfaction measure. *Leisure Sciences* 5(1):35-43.

Schomaker, J. H., and R. C. Knopf. 1982b. Generalization of a measure of visitor satisfaction with outdoor recreation. *Applied Psychological Measuement* 6(2):173-183.

Schreyer, R. 1980. Survey research in recreation management: Pitfalls and potentials. *Journal of Forestry* 78(6):338-340.

Schreyer, R., and R. C. Knopf. 1984. The dynamics of change in outdoor recreation environments—Some equity issues. *Journal of Park and Recreation Administration* 2(1):9-19.

Schreyer, R., and D. W. Lime. 1984. A novice isn't necessarily a novice—The influence of experience use history on subjective perceptions of recreation participation. *Leisure Sciences* 6(2):131-149.

Schreyer, R., D. W. Lime, and D. R. Williams. 1984. Characterizing the influence of past experience on recreation behavior. *Journal of Leisure Research* 16(1):34-50.

Schreyer, R., and J. W. Roggenbuck. 1978. The influence of experience expectations on crowding perceptions and social-psychological carrying capacities. *Leisure Sciences* 1(4):373-394.

Schreyer, R., and J. W. Roggenbuck. 1981. Visitor images of national parks: The influence of social definitions of places on perceptions and behavior. Pages 39-44 in: *Some Recent Products of River Recreation Research*. USDA Forest Service General Technical Report NC-63.

Schreyer, R., J. W. Roggenbuck, S. F. McCool, L. E. Royer, and J. Miller. 1976. *The Dinosaur National Monument Whitewater River Recreation Study*. Logan, Utah: Utah State University.

Schweitzer, D. L., and R. M. Randall. 1974. The key to getting research applied: Manager-researcher cooperation. *Journal of Forestry* 72:418-419.

Scotter, G. W. 1981. Response rates at unmanned trail registers, Waterton Lakes National Park, Alberta, Canada. *Journal of Leisure Research* 13(2):105-111.

Sessoms, H. D. 1961. *A Review of Selected Results of Recreation Studies*. Washington, D.C.: Outdoor Recreation Resources Review Commission.

Sessoms, H. D. 1963. An analysis of selected variables affecting outdoor recreation patterns. *Social Forces* 42(October):112-115.

Shafer, E. L., Jr. 1965. Socioeconomic characteristics of Adirondack campers. *Journal of Forestry* 63:690-694.

Shafer, E. L., Jr. 1969. *The Average Camper Who Doesn't Exist*. USDA Forest Service Research Paper NE-142.

Shafer, E. L., Jr., and H. D. Burke. 1965. Preferences for outdoor recreation facilities in four state parks. *Journal of Forestry* 63:512-518.

Shafer, E. L., Jr., and R. C. Lucas. 1979. Research needs and priorities for dispersed recreation management. *Journal of Leisure Research* 10(4):311-321.

Shafer, E. L., Jr., and J. Mietz. 1969. Aesthetic and emotional experiences rate high with northeastern wilderness hikers. *Environment and Behavior* 1(Dec.):187-197.

Shafer, E. L., Jr., and R. Thompson. 1968. Models that describe use of Adirondack campgrounds. *Forest Science* 14(4):383-391.

Schecter, M., and R. C. Lucas. 1978. *Simulation of Recreational Use for Park and Wilderness Management*. Baltimore, Maryland: Johns Hopkins University Press for Resources for the Future, Inc.

Shelby, B. 1980a. Crowding models for backcountry recreation. *Land Economics* 56(1):43-55.

Shelby, B. 1980b. Contrasting recreational experiences: Motors and oars in the Grand Canyon. *Journal of Soil and Water Conservation* 35(3):129-131.

Shelby, B. 1981a. Encounter norms in backcountry settings: Studies of three rivers. *Journal of Leisure Research* 13(2):129-138.

Shelby, B. 1981b. Research, politics, and resource management decisions: A case study of river research in Grand Canyon. *Leisure Sciences* 4(3):281-296.

Shelby, B., and R. Colvin. 1982. Encounter measures in carrying capacity research: Actual, reported and diary contacts. *Journal of Leisure Research* 14(4):350-360.

Shelby, B., M. S. Danley, K. C. Gibbs, and M. E. Petersen. 1982. Preferences of backpackers and river runners for allocation techniques. *Journal of Forestry* 80:416-419.

Shelby, B., and T. A. Heberlein. 1984. A conceptual framework for carrying capacity determination. *Leisure Sciences* 6(4):433-451.

Shelby, B., T. A. Heberlein, J. J. Vaske, and G. Alfano. 1983. Expectations, preferences, and feeling crowded in recreation activities. *Leisure Sciences* 6(1):1-14.

Shelby, B., D. Lowney, and P. McKee. 1980. Problems with satisfaction as a criterion for management and change. Paper presented at the annual meeting of the Rural Sociological Society, Ithaca, New York.

Sheridan, D. 1979. *Off-Road Vehicles on Public land.* Washington, D.C.: Council on Environmental Quality.

Smith, S., and W. W. Haythorn. 1972. The effects of compatibility, crowding, group size, and leadership seniority on stress, anxiety, hostility, and annoyance in isolated groups. *Journal of Personality and Social Psychology* 22(1):67-69.

Smith, S. L. 1975. Toward meta-recreation research. *Journal of Leisure Research* 7(Sum.):235-239.

Smith, V. K., and R. L. Headly. 1975. The use of computer simulation models in wilderness management. In: *Management Science Applications to Leisure Time* (S. Ladang, ed.). Amsterdam: North Holland.

Smith, V. K., and J. V. Krutilla. 1974. A simulation model for the management of low density recreational areas. *Journal of Environmental Economics and Management* 1:187-201.

Smith, V. K., and J. V. Krutilla. 1976. *Structure and Properties of a Wilderness Travel Simulator.* Baltimore: Johns Hopkins Press for Resources for the Future, Inc.

Sofranko, A. J., and M. F. Nolan. 1972. Early life experiences and adult sports participation. *Journal of Leisure Research* 4(Winter):6-18.

Solomon, M. J., and E. A. Hansen. 1972. *Canoeists' Suggestions for Stream Management in the Manistee National Forest in Michigan.* USDA Forest Service Research Paper NC-77.

Stankey, G. H. 1972. A strategy for the definition and management of wilderness quality. Pages 88-114 in: *Natural Environments: Studies in Theoretical and Applied Analysis* (J. V. Krutilla, ed.). Baltimore: The Johns Hopkins University Press.

Stankey, G. H. 1973. *Visitor Perception of Wilderness Recreation Carrying Capacity.* USDA Forest Service Research Paper INT-142.

Stankey, G. H. 1974. Criteria for the determination of recreational carrying capacity in the Colorado River Basin. In: *Environmental Management in The Colorado River Basin* (A. B. Crawford and D. F. Peterson, eds.). Logan, Utah: Utah State University Press.

Stankey, G. H. 1979. Use rationing in two southern California wildernesses. *Journal of Forestry* 77(5):347-349.

Stankey, G. H. 1980a. *A Comparison of Carrying Capacity Perceptions Among Visitors to Two Wildernesses.* USDA Forest Service Research Paper INT-242.

Stankey, G. H. 1980b. Wilderness carrying capacity: Management and research progress in the United States. *Landscape Research* 5(3):6-11.

Stankey, G. H. 1980c. Integrating wildland recreation research into decisionmaking: Pitfalls and promises. Pages 43-56 in: *Symposium Proceedings: Applied Research for Parks and Recreation in the 1980s.* University of Victoria, Victoria, British Columbia, Canada.

Stankey, G. H., and J. Baden. 1977. *Rationing Wilderness Use: Methods, Problems, and Guidelines.* USDA Forest Service Research Paper INT-192.

Stankey, G. H., D. N. Cole, R. C. Lucas, M. E. Petersen, S. S. Frissell, and R. F. Washburne. 1985. *The Limits of Acceptable Change (LAC) System for Wilderness Planning.* USDA Forest Service General Technical Report INT-176.

Stankey, G. H., and D. W. Lime. 1973. *Recreational Carrying Capacity: An Annotated Bibliography.* USDA Forest Service General Technical Report INT-3.

Stankey, G. H., R. C. Lucas, and D. W. Lime. 1976. Crowding in parks and wilderness. *Design and Environment* 7(3):38-41.

Stankey, G. H., R. C. Lucas, and R. Ream. 1973. Relationships between hunting success and satisfaction. Pages 77-84 in: *Proceedings of the Thirty-Eighth North American Wildlife and Natural Resources Conference.* The Wildlife Management Institute, Washington, D.C.

Stankey, G. H., and S. F. McCool. 1984. Carrying capacity in recreational settings: Evaluation, appraisal, and application. *Leisure Sciences* 6(4):453-473.

Stankey, G. H., S. F. McCool, and G. C. Stokes. 1984. Limits of acceptable change: A new framework for managing the Bob Marshall Wilderness Complex. *Western Wildlands* 10(3):33-37.

Stokols, D. 1972a. On the distinction between density and crowding: Some implications for future research. *Psychological Review* 79(3):275-277.

Stokols, D. 1972b. A social psychological model of human crowding phenomena. *Journal of American Institute of Planners* 38:72-83.

Stynes, D. J. 1982. The role of information in recreation site selection. Pages 100-104 in: *Forest and River Recreation: Research Update.* University of Minnesota Agricultural Experiment Station Miscellaneous Publication 18.

Stynes, D. J., M. I. Bevins, and T. L. Brown. 1980. Trends or methodological differences? Pages 223-231 in: *Proceedings of the 1980 Outdoor Recreation Trends Symposium, Volume I.* USDA Forest Service General Technical Report NE-57.

Sumner, E. L. 1936. Special report on a wildlife study in the High Sierra in Sequoia and Yosemite National Parks and adjacent territory. Unpublished report, U.S. National Park Service Records, National Archives, Washington, D.C.

Tarbet, D., G. H. Moeller, and K. T. McLoughlin. 1977. Attitudes of Salmon River users toward management of wild and scenic rivers. Pages 365-371 in: *River Recreation Management and Research Symposium.* USDA Forest Service General Technical Report NC-28.

Thomas, L. G. 1956. Leisure pursuits by socio-economic strata. *Journal of Educational Sociology* 29:367-377.

Tinsley, H. E. A. 1984. Limitations, explorations, aspirations: A confession of fallibility and a promise to strive for perfection. *Journal of Leisure Research* 16(2):93-98.

Tinsley, H. E. A., T. C. Barrett, and R. A. Kass. 1977. Leisure activities and need satisfaction. *Journal of Leisure Research* 92(2):110-120.

Tinsley, H. E. A., and T. L. Johnson. 1984. A preliminary taxonomy of leisure activities. *Journal of Leisure Research* 16(3):234-244.

Tinsley, H. E. A., and R. A. Kass. 1978. Sex effects in the study of leisure activities and need satisfaction: A replication and extension. *Journal of Leisure Research* 10:191-202.

Tinsley, H. E. A., and R. A. Kass. 1979. The latent structure of the need satisfying properties of leisure activities. *Journal of Leisure Research* 11(4):278-291.

Titre, J., and A. S. Mills. 1982. Effect of encounters on perceived crowding and satisfaction. Pages 146-153 in: *Forest and River Recreation: Research Update*. University of Minnesota Agricultural Experiment Station Miscellaneous Publication 18.

Towler, W. L. 1977. Hiker perception of wilderness: A study of the social carrying capacity of Grand Canyon. *Arizona Review* 26(8-9):1-10.

Twight, B. W., and W. R. Catton, Jr. 1975. The politics of images: Forest managers versus recreation publics. *Natural Resources Journal* 15(2):297-306.

Twight, B. W., K. L. Smith, and G. H. Wassinger. 1981. Privacy and camping: Closeness to the self vs. closeness to others. *Leisure Sciences* 4(4):427-441.

Utter, J., W. Gleason, and S. F. McCool. 1981. User perceptions of river recreation allocation techniques. Pages 27-32 in: *Some Recent Products of River Recreation Research*. USDA Forest Service General Technical Report NC-63.

Valins, S., and A. Baum. 1973. Residential group size, social interaction and crowding. *Environment and Behavior* 5(4):421-440.

VanWagtendonk, J. W. 1980. Visitor use patterns in Yosemite National Park. *Journal of Travel Research* 19(2):12-17.

VanWagtendonk, J. W. 1981. The effect of use limits on backcountry visitation trends in Yosemite National Park. *Leisure Sciences* 4(3):311-323.

VanWagtendonk, J. W., and J. M. Benedict. 1980. Wilderness permit compliance and validity. *Journal of Forestry* 78(7):399-401.

Vaske, J. J., M. P. Donnelly, and T. A. Heberlein. 1980. Perceptions of crowding and resource quality by early and more recent visitors. *Leisure Sciences* 3:367-381.

Vaske, J. J., A. R. Graefe, and A. Dempster. 1982. Social and environmental influences on perceived crowding. Pages 211-227 in: *Proceedings of The Wilderness Psychology Group Conference*. West Virginia University, Morgantown.

Vaux, H. J., Jr. 1975. The distribution of income among wilderness users. *Journal of Leisure Research* 7(1):29-37.

Veblen, T. 1912. *Theory of the Leisure Class*. New York: Macmillan.

Wagar, J. A. 1963. *Campgrounds for Many Tastes*. USDA Forest Service Research Paper INT-6.

Wagar, J. A. 1964. *The Carrying Capacity of Wild Lands for Recreation*. Forest Science Monograph 7, Society of American Foresters, Washington, D.C.

Wagar, J. A. 1966. Quality in outdoor recreation. *Trends* 3(3):9-12.

Wagar, J. A. 1968. The place of carrying capacity in the management of recreation lands. In: *Third Annual Rocky Mountain-High Plains Park and Recreation Conference Proceedings*. Colorado State University, Fort Collins, Colorado.

Wagar, J. A. 1969. *Estimation of Visitor Use from Self-Registration at Developed Recreation Sites*. USDA Forest Service Research Paper INT-70.

Wagar, J. A. 1974. Recreational carrying capacity reconsidered. *Journal of Forestry* 72:274-278.

Wagar, J. A., and J. F. Thalheimer. 1969. *Trial Results of Net Count Procedures for Estimating Visitor Use at Developed Recreation Sites*. USDA Forest Service Research Note INT-105.

Wagar, J. V. K. 1946. Services and facilities for forest recreationists. *Journal of Forestry* 44(11):883-887.

Wagar, J. V. K. 1951. Some major principles in recreation land use planning. *Journal of Forestry* 49:431-435.

Washburne, R. F. 1981. Carrying capacity assessment and recreational use in the national wilderness preservation system. *Journal of Soil and Water Conservation* 36(3):162-166.

Washburne, R. F. 1982. Wilderness recreational carrying capacity: Are numbers necessary? *Journal of Forestry* 80(Nov.):726-728.

Washburne, R. F., and D. N. Cole. 1983. *Problems and Practices in Wilderness Management: A Survey of Managers*. USDA Forest Service Research Paper INT-304.

Webb, E. J., D. T. Campbell, R. D. Schwartz, and L. Sechrest. 1966. *Unobtrusive Measures: Nonreactive Research in the Social Sciences*. Chicago: Rand McNally and Company.

Wellman, J. D., M. S. Dawson, and J. W. Roggenbuck. 1982. Park managers predictions of the motivations of visitors to two national park areas. *Journal of Leisure Research* 14(1):1-15.

Wenger, W. D., Jr. 1964. *A Test of Unmanned Registration Stations on Wilderness Trails: Factors Influencing Effectiveness*. USDA Forest Service Research Paper PNW-16.

Wenger, W. D., Jr., and H. M. Gregersen. 1964. *The Effect of Non-Response on Representativeness of Wilderness-Trail Register Information*. USDA Forest Service Research Paper PNW-17.

Wenger, W. D., Jr., and R. Videbeck. 1969. Eye pupillary measurement of aesthetic response to forest scenes. *Journal of Leisure Research* 1(2):149-162.

West, P. C. 1977. A status group dynamics approach to predicting participation rates in regional recreation demand studies. *Land Economics* 53:196-211.

West, P. C. 1981a. *On-Site Social Surveys and the Determination of Social Carrying Capacity in Wildland Recreation Management*. USDA Forest Service Research Note NC-264.

West, P. C. 1981b. Perceived crowding and attitudes toward limiting use in backcountry recreation areas. *Leisure Sciences* 4(4):419-426.

West, P. C. 1982a. A nationwide test of the status group dynamics approach to outdoor recreation demand. *Leisure Sciences* 5(1):1-18.

West, P. C. 1982b. Effects of user behavior on the perception of crowding in backcountry forest recreation. *Forest Science* 28(1):95-105.

West, P. C. 1983. A test of the projection accuracy of the status group dynamic approach to recreation demand. *Leisure Sciences* 6(1):15-45.

West, P. C. 1984. Status differences and interpersonal influence in the adoption of outdoor recreation activities. *Journal of Leisure Research* 16(4):350-354.

West, P. C., and L. C. Merriam, Jr. 1970. Outdoor recreation and family cohesiveness: A research approach. *Journal of Leisure Research* 2(4):251-259.

Westin, A. F. 1967. *Privacy and Freedom*. New York: Atheneum Books.

White, R. C. 1955. Social class differences in the uses of leisure. *American Journal of Sociology* 61(2):145-150.

Wicker, A. W. 1969. Attitudes versus actions: The relationship of verbal and overt behavioral responses to attitude objects. *Journal of Social Issues* 25(4):41-78.

Wildland Research Center, University of California. 1962. *Wilderness and Recreation—A Report on Resources, Values, and Problems*. Outdoor Recreation Resources Review Commission Study Report 3. Washington, D.C.: U.S. Government Printing Office.

Willis, C. E., J. J. Canavan, and R. S. Bond. 1975. Optimal short-run pricing policies for a public campground. *Journal of Leisure Research* 7(2):108-113.

Witt, P. A. 1971. Factor structure of leisure behavior for high school age youth in three communities. *Journal of Leisure Research* 3(4):213-220.

Witt, P. A., and D. W. Bishop. 1970. Situational antecedents to leisure behavior. *Journal of Leisure Research* 2(1):64-77.

Witter, D. J., P. S. Haverland, L. C. Belusz, and C. E. Hicks. 1982. Missouri trout park anglers: Their motives and opinions of management. Pages 69-73 in: *Forest and River Recreation: Research Update*. University of Minnesota Agricultural Experiment Station Miscellaneous Report 18.

Wohlwill, J. F., and H. Heft. 1977. A comparative study of user attitudes towards development and facilities in two contrasting natural recreation areas. *Journal of Leisure Research* 9(4):264-280.

Womble, P., and S. Studebaker. 1981. Crowding in a national park campground. *Environment and Behavior* 13(5):557-573.

Yoesting, D. R., and D. L. Burkhead. 1973. Significance of childhood recreation experience on adult leisure behavior: An exploratory analysis. *Journal of Leisure Research* 5(Winter):25-36.

Yoesting, D. R., and J. E. Christensen. 1978. Reexamining the significance of childhood recreation patterns on adult leisure behavior. *Leisure Sciences* 1(3):219-229.

Index